Praise for *Cut-Th*

CW01497164

In business, you don't get what you deserve – you get what you pitch for. That's why I've always taught entrepreneurs that the first skill to master is pitching. *Cut-Through* is a masterclass in doing exactly that. Dominic Colenso has taken years of stage experience, coaching, and neuroscience and distilled it into a powerful, practical playbook. Whether you're selling an idea, a product, or a vision for the future, this book will sharpen your message and boost your impact. Essential reading for anyone who wants to be heard.

> — **Daniel Priestley**
> **Founder of Dent Global and award-winning entrepreneur**
> **Best-selling author of *Key Person of Influence***

Cut-Through is an indispensable guide for anyone looking to truly master the art of impactful communication. Dominic is always adept at offering a practical and actionable framework to help structure the approach to communicating effectively – and this book is no different. He expertly demystifies the process of creating engaging pitches and presentations, elevating what might seem an innate talent into a learnable skill. This book provides the definitive roadmap to ensure your message not only resonates but leaves a lasting impression with the audience and gets the desired result. It's a must-read for elevating your influence.

> — **Chris Wynn**
> **Director of Communications**
> **John Lewis Partnership**

Clarity, confidence, and authenticity – these define performances by top actors. An entire industry now exists to help entrepreneurs and businesses tap into the same qualities that allow great performers to compel our attention. Drawing on his impressive track record as an actor and director, Dominic Colenso has distilled this landscape into a guide that is both comprehensive and succinct. This book 'unpicks' the core elements of great performance – rehearsing, bringing words to life, and perhaps most importantly, listening – making the path to confident, convincing presenting, and pitching clear and accessible to all. Read on!

— **Ellis Jones**
  Former Vice Principle and Head of Acting
  Royal Academy of Dramatic Art

Cut-Through is the playbook every sales professional needs in today's noisy world. Dominic nails what it really takes to capture attention and convert it into action – with zero fluff and 100% practical value. His Six Ds framework is smart, simple, and immediately usable. I've seen Dom in action, and what he teaches isn't theory – it works. If you want to win more pitches, have more impactful conversations, and genuinely stand out from the competition, this book will show you how. Read it, apply it, and watch what happens.

— **Tony Morris**
  International Sales Speaker
  Author of *Coffee's for Closers*

Building on the foundations of *IMPACT*, Dominic Colenso delivers another masterclass in embodied communication. *Cut-Through* transforms the art of pitching and presenting through his unique blend of theatrical expertise and business acumen. The Six Ds methodology doesn't just teach technique – it engages the whole human in bringing logic, human connection, creativity, and action (head, heart, gut, and feet) to each and every presentation.

As a performance coach, I witness daily how poor delivery undermines brilliant ideas. This book bridges that gap with no-nonsense frameworks that build confidence from the inside out. Whether facing boardrooms or cameras, Dominic's approach develops the whole performer, not just the presentation.

— **Dr Claire Dale**
  Founder Director, Physical Intelligence Institute and
  Companies in Motion
  Author of *Physical Intelligence*

I've worked with Dominic for over 15 years, and there's a reason I keep going back – he's the best in the business when it comes to developing real-world communication skills. Whether you're a future leader or a seasoned executive, the ability to pitch, present, and truly connect with an audience is critical – and *Cut-Through* delivers the playbook every professional needs. This isn't theory – it's a toolkit for personal growth and organisational impact.

— **Nick Walker**
  VP People and Workplace
  Bolt

This playbook is an indispensable guide for anyone wishing to make their ideas heard and remembered. Following on from his book *IMPACT*, Dominic once again provides practical tools on not just how to present but how to connect with your audience. Whether you're pitching a bold vision or crafting an important presentation, this book will help you cut through and have the impact you want.

— **Craig Watkins**
  CEO
  Verian UK

As someone who doesn't consider himself a natural presenter, Dominic's *IMPACT* framework gave me the confidence to step up and deliver with far greater clarity and presence. *Cut-Through* takes that to the next level. This book is an essential playbook for anyone in sales looking to communicate with more purpose, energy, and influence. Presentations and pitches are the heartbeat of our profession – yet too few sales professionals invest the time to truly master them. Dominic gives you the structure and mindset to stand out when it matters most.

— **Steve Lindsey**
Managing Director
Lincoln West and National Sales Conference

Cut-Through gets straight to the point – and shows you how to do the same. It's full of tools, insights, and stories that actually work in the real world. As someone who's led global communications and worked across multiple stakeholder groups, I really appreciate how Dominic combines strategy with simplicity and storytelling. Whether you're in the boardroom or pitching to a client, this book will help you land your message with impact.

— **Catherine Keogh**
Chief Corporate Affairs Officer
Kerry Group

Colenso's ideas are dangerous. He draws you in with a charmingly anecdotal style, so that you don't even realize that you have been sucked into his unique 6Ds approach. And then he gradually reveals a treasure trove of practical techniques that great speakers and actors have kept secret for hundreds of years. So please don't buy the book, as it may put me out of business.

— **Graham Davies**
Author of *The Presentation Coach*

When we cast Dominic in *Thunderbirds*, I watched him realize the opportunity he had just been given. The late great Bill Paxton played his father and Sir Ben Kingsley played the delicious villain The Hood. The lessons Dom wisely took from these pros have served him well. The discipline of rehearsal and energy of performance has been translated into *Cut-Through: The pitch and presentation playbook*. It's smart, structured, and refreshingly human.

— **Jonathan Frakes**
  Actor and Director
  'Commander Riker' – *Star Trek: The Next Generation*

DOMINIC COLENSO

CUT ⟶
THROUGH

THE PITCH AND PRESENTATION PLAYBOOK

First published in Great Britain by Practical Inspiration Publishing, 2026

ISBN   9781788608367 (paperback)
        9781788608350 (hardback)
        9781788608374 (epub)

EU GPSR representative: LOGOS EUROPE, 9 rue Nicolas Poussin, LA ROCHELLE 17000, France Contact@logoseurope.eu

Want to bulk-buy copies of this book for your team and colleagues? We can customize the content and co-brand *Cut-Through* to suit your business's needs.

Please email info@practicalinspiration.com for more details.

Practical Inspiration Publishing

MIX
Paper | Supporting responsible forestry
FSC
www.fsc.org   FSC® C013604

For Laura and Nell,
still my reasons why.

Contents

Chapter Two
DISTIL: Cut it back to the core 47

Chapter Three
DESIGN: Craft a blockbuster narrative 79

Foreword

Before I tell you why you must read Dominic's book, let me tell you when. You walk off stage or out of the meeting room, and the sick feeling in your stomach tells you what the audience already knows: you didn't land it.

Truth be told, this feeling is more familiar than you'd like to admit. It leaves you anxious and pretty darn miserable. You know you can do better, so why aren't you?

You have the breakthrough idea. You're passionate about your message. You know why it matters to your audience. Your story doesn't suck, but you do. (Your mum won't tell you, but the audience's silence just did.) This is precisely when you need to read Dominic's book, because you have all the ingredients for a cut-through pitch or presentation, but you don't yet understand how to put them together: the right order, the right timing, and crucially, what to leave out.

After 16 years of running *The Do Lectures* and witnessing hundreds of talks that have garnered over 150 million views online, I've learned something fundamental: Structure is everything.

The good news? There's a subtle art to it. The even better news? It can be learned. This is why you need Dominic's book.

It solves your presentation structure problems in simple, practical steps.

First, it answers: how can I keep this simple?

Most talks try to say too much and end up saying very little. In a world addicted to noise, Dominic's quiet revolution is clear: know thy outcome. What is the one idea you want them to remember? What is the one feeling you want them to walk away with? What is the one action you want them to take?

There is an invisible wall between you and your audience. You climb over that wall by saying less – but making it mean more.

The second question it answers is: how do I get to clarity fast?

I've seen too many speakers tell the story before the story before the actual story. 'Once upon a time, I had breakfast... Then lunch... '. They take the long way around, and in my head, I'm begging: *get to the point*.

I've seen speakers leave out the entire backstory so the main story makes no sense, and, they're still mystified when it doesn't land.

I've seen speakers talk passionately for over an hour only for the audience to ask afterwards, 'So, what exactly is it you do?'.

Clarity is a superpower precisely because it's so rare.

When I started Hiut Denim Co, I knew our story was about rebirth. It was the story of a town that had Britain's largest jeans factory, which closed in 2002, leaving 400 unemployed. My opening line in every pitch and presentation became: 'My town is making jeans again'. That single sentence contained everything.

Clarity isn't volume. It's precision. Dominic's book teaches you how to communicate with this kind of clarity.

Third, why Dominic?

When I'm learning something crucial, I seek teachers who've performed at the highest level and possess an uncommon edge. Dominic has both.

Dominic began his career as a professional actor, working extensively on stage and screen, before training as a director at the Royal Academy of Dramatic Art in London.

He's appeared in BBC period dramas and big-budget Hollywood films. He's best known for playing Virgil Tracy in the Hollywood adaptation of *Thunderbirds*, alongside Bill Paxton and Sir Ben Kingsley.

He knows how to deliver under pressure, when the spotlight shines in his face, and there's nowhere to hide.

How do you breathe? How do you rehearse to remember everything clearly? How do you deliver precisely when the pressure is highest?

Dominic has done this at an elite level. Now, he shares his unique insights with you in this book.

One of the most valuable skills you can learn is to relax deeply precisely when you care the most. Learning how not to freeze is a forever skill.

Though I've watched hundreds of talks, and delivered keynotes for Apple, Google, Facebook, Pinterest, and more, I often find myself returning to Dominic's YouTube channel, taking endless notes. Now, thankfully, he's distilled those invaluable lessons into this essential book.

It's essential for one simple reason: because your business, your idea, your story is often just one cut-through presentation away from changing everything.

This is not a book – it's a lifeboat.

David Hieatt
Co-Founder of The Do Lectures and Hiut Denim Co
Author of *Do Purpose*

Preface
It starts with silence

It's 10:49 on Monday 16 December, 2024, and I'm sitting in a tiny cottage, in a picturesque village in the Yorkshire Dales, England, writing the first words of this book. The only sounds I can hear are the wind rustling the trees outside the window, the dog breathing in his basket and my own fingers striking the keys of the keyboard. I'm nestled on the sofa, surrounded by the works of some of my favourite authors, sticky notes strewn about me. A cafetière of freshly brewed coffee is standing on the coffee table. My phone is on silent, my email out-of-office is on, and my loved ones have strict instructions to contact me only if there's a life-threatening emergency.

This moment is not accidental.

It's borne of months of planning, countless conversations with friends and mentors and hundreds of hours of thinking and daydreaming about the words now flowing onto the page.

Why so drastic? Why so strategic? Why not more spontaneous and fun?

The simple answer is distraction. The overwhelm of information that interrupts our thinking on a continual basis.

Our best work starts with silence.

If we want our words to have what I will refer to throughout this book as 'cut-through', if we want to stand out and be memorable, we must get ruthlessly clear on exactly what we want to say. If we're not focused, we can't expect our audience to be.

Let's be honest: I'm not expecting for a second that every time you have an important presentation or pitch to prepare, you run to a cabin in the woods. As romantic as it sounds, it's completely impractical. Instead, I want to offer you a simple playbook, a practical guide for approaching these important moments with more clarity and certainty. A way of structuring your thinking and planning your preparation that will make you more successful.

My hope is that in the pages that follow you'll discover an effective set of tools that will help you capture and hold your audience's attention, increasing your influence, your confidence and ultimately allowing you to deliver a winning performance.

Let's dive in.

Introduction

Why life's a pitch

The problem with pitches and presentations

Life's a pitch.

The pun is intentional but I'm also deadly serious.

Every conversation you have, every email you send, every meeting you attend is an opportunity to craft your future. Sometimes in a tiny, inconspicuous way. Sometimes in a blindingly obvious, earth-shatteringly huge way.

Dramatic but true.

How we communicate has a massive impact on the trajectory of our lives. It shapes our relationships and our outcomes, both personal and professional.

But not all moments of communication are created equal.

The most formal formats are pitches and presentations. They're normally where the stakes are highest, where the opportunities are greatest and the potential for failure is at its most pronounced. We might be trying to make a sale or close a deal. We might be trying to get buy-in from our boss, get funding for a project or get our colleagues to adopt a new way of working. We might be trying to convince investors to part with their cash or to convince a loved one to support our new idea.

These pitches and presentations can be life changing and yet we must face a simple truth: most pitches and presentations suck.

From the moment we're old enough to enter the classroom, to the moment we finally retire and walk out of the workplace (and potentially beyond!) we're continually subjected to the monotony of slide after slide, packed full of information, delivered in a way that makes us want to bang our head against the desk.

Pitches and presentations are often an afterthought or something that's rushed. They could be a brain dump into a slide deck, or worse, a duplicate of a previous document hastily tweaked with a few new graphs and an updated title page. Even serious sales and investment pitches can seem ill-prepared, delivered in language that doesn't resonate with the prospect and fails to hold people's attention for more than a few seconds.

The first presentation I ever remember giving was the culmination of a term-long primary school project on the topic of 'France'. I was nine years old.

On the day in question, 27 of my classmates and I gathered in the cramped school library for an afternoon of show and tell. It was 1990. My dad was a sales director for a chemical company and in order to prepare for my moment in the spotlight I had raided his briefcase and stolen eight transparent films to use on the school's overhead projector.

For those reading this book born after 1995, an 'OHP' as it was known, was, at the time, as cutting edge as a 3D hologram. My excitement at being able to use it for my presentation was off the charts. Essentially a box with a light in it, attached to a magnifying glass and a mirror, you wrote or drew in permanent marker on sheets of transparent plastic which you then placed on the light box only for what you had written to be magically projected onto the wall or screen in front of you. Assuming of course that you'd placed the plastic sheet the right way up. Otherwise, the whole thing appeared backwards!

Not only did I have slides, I also had an actual telescopic pointing stick. I was in full-on 90s executive mode! However, I also had something else with me which later proved to be a secret weapon.

As much as it pains me to admit it, my presentation was pretty boring. As I placed each slide on the projector and read what was written verbatim, my classmates stared into space or out of the window. Despite my own fascination with the topic, no-one else seemed to care at all. I'd lost my audience. My presentation career was over.

Then, completely unexpectedly, something magical happened.

After displaying a particularly detailed map of gastronomic delicacies produced in the south of the country I reached into my bag and pulled out a box of cheese. More specifically, 250g of Roquefort blue ewe's cheese cut into tiny chunks.

All of a sudden people sat up. Their eyes fixated on me, hanging on every word until the moment arrived to sample the goods. What ensued was a kaleidoscope of reactions. From those with more sophisticated taste buds enjoying the salty tang and sour finish, to those with a more normal nine-year-old palette fighting for the wastepaper bin to spit out the offending morsels.

Thirty-five years on, several of my classmates still recall the presentation. I had unwittingly achieved the holy grail of cut-through but probably for the wrong reasons!

I'm not of course suggesting for a second that good pitches or presentations require dairy-based props. Or that unless you provoke a violent reaction in your audience, what you're saying will never be memorable. But if we want our message to live on in the hearts and minds of our audience, we need to find a way to stand out from the crowd. We need to occupy space in the memories of those listening to us, not just in the moment but in the hours, days and weeks after the pitch or presentation is over. This book aims to show you how.

Living in an AHA world

The world has changed a lot since my first encounter with an overhead projector. And so has the volume of information that the average human being consumes. Back then, my family's PC had a 40-megabyte hard drive. By contrast the most recent twelve-minute YouTube video I created was 1.8 gigabytes! But it's not just a size thing. It's a volume thing too. We're bombarded by a continuous stream of content competing for our attention. Instant messages, emails, videos, memes. Everywhere we turn something else is fighting for our focus.

As much as we might like to think we're less distracted during work hours, the data disagrees. In fact, in a 2023 Microsoft survey[1] of 31,000 people, across 31 countries, 68% of people said they didn't have enough uninterrupted focus time during the workday.

We live in what I often refer to as an AHA world. AI focused, Hyperconnected and Always-On.

Given the speed with which large language model artificial intelligences like ChatGPT are developing, it's clear that the battle for our audience's engagement is only going to get more competitive.

Words and videos generated by robots are surreptitiously filling our social feeds. It's already commonplace for people to offer AI a series of bullet points and ask it to craft them into an email or message in a particular tone.

What's even more mind blowing is that it's also not uncommon for the recipient of that message to then take it and run it though their own AI software to reduce it back down to a series of bullet points again.

We run the risk of what should be transformational communication being reduced to the transactional. But rather than the proliferation of AI content being cause for concern, I think it offers us a massive opportunity. Those who can harness the power of their unique human voice will reap the rewards. In a sea of sameness, there is a chance to stand out.

It's hard to get away from the noise. We're rarely more than arm's length from our smartphones and it's (unfortunately) no longer universally considered rude to have one eye on your device whilst the person in front of you is talking. I've lost track of the number of presentations I've sat through where half the audience appears to be reading something more compelling or urgent on their laptop or tablet. Again, it's easy to get downhearted by this behaviour. But the smarter choice is to notice what's happening and to do something about it.

With the opportunity for digital connectivity lasting from the moment we open our eyes in the morning to the moment we close them again in the evening, the stage is set for an epic battle. It's no longer good enough to be competent. Having a well-designed slide deck will only get you so far. Even a great story on its own is unlikely to get your audience fully onboard.

Instead, if you want your words not just to land but to hold your audience's focus, leaving them ready to act and desperate for more, you have to create a rare and powerful thing. You have to create a moment of cut-through that stops your audience in their tracks and delivers you their undivided attention.

But what does cut-through even mean?

Creating cut-through

There are some people in life we feel compelled to listen to. There's something about the way they deliver their message that draws us in. Interestingly, when we look deeper, the detail of what they say seems to be less important than their delivery and their ability to capture an idea in a simple way.

The world is full of influencers, politicians and celebrities that – when you scratch beneath the surface – have remarkably little to say but nevertheless have scores of people queuing up to hear them say it. Rather than get frustrated by this conundrum, we need to learn from it. In almost every line of work, whether we're salespeople, managers or leaders, trying to influence our friends, our families or our boss, we want what those lucky few get: cut-through.

The Cambridge English Dictionary defines cut-through as 'success in getting people's attention and influencing them'.[2] The aim of a great pitch or presentation should be nothing more and nothing less.

Of course, you need to strive for more than just soundbites and clickbait. If there's no substance to your message people will quickly be distracted by the next shiny thing. But cut-through is the Trojan Horse. It gives you a foot in the door and gifts you the possibility of opening your audience to what comes next.

In their book *Smart Brevity*, Jim VandeHei, Mike Allen and Rory Schwartz, co-founders of media platform Axios encourage us to 'adapt to how people consume content – not how you wish they did or they did once upon a time. Then change how you communicate immediately'.[3] It's sound advice.

The world of presentations and pitching has changed little in the last few decades. Yes, we have moved on from overhead projectors, but for the most part, people's approaches have remained largely unchanged. And that's not a good thing.

If we look instead at the world of my former career as a TV and film actor, the contrast is stark. Go back and find a drama made 30 years ago and the majority of them will feel plodding and ponderous. I loved the BBC series *All Creatures Great and Small* as a child and back then I was completely captivated. Revisiting it now, it appears painfully slow. The FX series *The Bear* by contrast is like being on a rollercoaster. The choppy editing and searing soundtrack left me feeling, in moments, quite unable to breathe. News available 24 hours, overflowing social media feeds and incessant digital marketing have primed the modern human brain for a different type of engagement.

Rather than resisting, we need to learn to adapt. The first thing to embrace is emotion.

Emotion is the currency of attention, and it stops distraction in its tracks. If you can make your audience feel something, if you can leave them in a different emotional state at the end of your interaction compared to where they were at the beginning, you have earned the right to be remembered. You have taken the first step towards cutting through the noise.

However, emotion alone is not enough. The second element required to create cut-through is simplicity. Complexity is a sure-fire way to lose your audience. Instead, you need to be able to take complicated ideas and deliver them in a way that is easy to understand.

Without straying into politics, there is a clear trend at present for simple slogans and phrases of as few words as possible. At least initially, audiences don't seem to have an appetite for detail, they want to connect with the high-level concept before they will entertain the nuance. That means you need to aim for economy. The simpler your message, the more likely it is to land.

Finally, to ensure that you leave a lasting impression, the third element needed for cut-through is energy. You must be seen to believe in what you're saying, otherwise you can't expect others to. Energy in a pitch or presentation context may seem somewhat intangible but as an audience member you know when you're on the receiving end of it. As a presenter it's your job to find the right energy to breathe life into your ideas.

Emotion. Simplicity. Energy. If you want to create cut-through, you need to bring these three elements together in every pitch

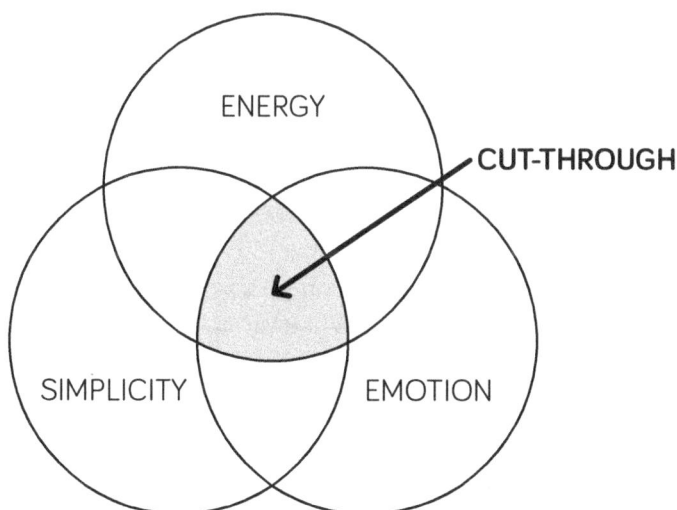

Figure 1 The cut-through sweet spot

and presentation you deliver. They are the secret sauce. Their intersection is the sweet spot you should be aiming for. The ideas I'm about to share will give you a methodology for cultivating them.

If you want your pitches and presentations to have the greatest likelihood of making an impact, you can't leave things up to chance. Instead, I'd encourage you to approach the task more strategically and methodically.

What you need is a playbook.

Why you need a playbook

For over 15 years I've been working with businesses on their communication skills. At first it was something I did to supplement my acting income, but it quickly developed into an obsession. For the last 11 years it's been my full-time job.

Over that decade, I've lost count of the number of presentations I've sat through and critiqued. From delivering presentation skills courses to graduates, to sitting round the boardroom table coaching senior leaders on pitches worth millions, I've had the chance to observe the good, the bad and the ugly.

What I've discovered is a pattern. A way of approaching the task that dramatically increases the chances of success. Of course, there's no way to guarantee the outcome, but if certain steps are omitted the likelihood of failure dramatically increases.

Naturally, success is measured differently in different contexts. It may be as simple as positive feedback from your peers on your contribution in a meeting, or as complex as securing the purchase order for a seven-figure deal. Whatever it looks like to you, if you want to increase the odds of achieving it, the approach I've developed and tested globally with thousands of clients across a wide spectrum of industries and sectors can help.

Back in 2019 I published my first book *IMPACT: How to be more confident, increase your influence and know what to say under pressure*.[4]

The IMPACT methodology I shared in those pages is at the heart of everything I do. Six ingredients for successful communication in any situation.

I INTENTION

The I is Intention. Whenever we communicate, we need to, in the words of the late, great leadership expert Steven Covey 'begin with the end in mind'.[5] Setting a clear intention allows you to know if you're heading towards or away from your target. You need to get clear on what you want your audience to know, feel and do once you're done.

M MINDSET

The M is Mindset. Most of us hear voices in our heads. The problem is that this evolutionary response – designed to keep us safe – is rarely an internal cheerleader when the stakes are high. Instead, it finds fault in our performance and encourages us to play safe. We need to take control of what's going on between our own ears if we want our message to land.

P PRESENCE

The P is Presence. As an actor a key part of my performance was what I did with my body and my voice. It turns out all those things I learned in movement and speech classes are backed up by neuroscience and are just as applicable in the real world. If you want your audience to trust you, you need to look and sound credible.

A AUDIENCE

The A is Audience. Who are you speaking to and how do you speak their language? It's tempting to look at the world through a single lens and ignore other people's perspectives. The best communicators however are those who understand how to flex their style and step into their audience's shoes. They avoid the trap of making everything about themselves and focus instead on making their message resonate for others.

 CONTENT

The C is Content. This is the 'what' of your communication, the message you are trying to convey. In pitches and presentations, it's your visual story as well as your spoken one. One of the hardest things to do as an actor is to accurately learn your lines. When working with people in business I actively discourage it. Instead, I advocate the use of frameworks to help you craft a compelling narrative.

 TECHNIQUE

And finally, the T is Technique. The word authenticity is often overused but it's vital to successful communication. No one wants to see you pretending to be someone else, they want to see you being the best version of you. Just like any elite performer, the best presenters spend time honing their skill, putting in the private practice to make the public display seem effortless. There are no shortcuts, but the hard work does pay off.

If you've read *IMPACT* every word in this book connects to one of those six ingredients. What I'm about to share with you doesn't negate anything that came before. In fact, it is designed to build seamlessly on the foundations I laid within those pages but to deal more specifically and in greater detail with the art of pitching and presenting. If you've yet to read *IMPACT*, you can add it to your wishlist safe if the knowledge that no previous understanding of it is necessary to extract maximum value from the pages that follow.

Actors, or players, capture their audience's imagination and take them on a journey. The best presenters do the same. They educate and entertain. Even the most technical topics can be delivered in a compelling way, as long as the person delivering the message is willing to play. *Cut-Through* is a playbook in multiple senses of the word. This 'playbook' is a collection of strategies, methods and processes to help you deliver a winning performance. But it is also a 'play' book – an encouragement to approach the topic with a sense of fun and childlike curiosity.

As an audience member at the theatre or the cinema, when we lose ourselves in a performance, we believe the actor is speaking the words for the first time, finding the inspiration for their thoughts in the moment. The reality, of course, couldn't be further from the truth. Behind the scenes something much more structured and strategic is taking place.

When we approach the craft of pitching and presenting, we need a structured and strategic approach too.

Let me introduce you to the six Ds.

The six Ds

A pitch is a presentation, and a presentation is a pitch.

There are differences of course. A traditional pitch is more sales focused, whereas a traditional presentation is normally about disseminating an idea. But ultimately, they're built on the same foundations.

For brevity I will use the terms interchangeably throughout this book.

Whatever the label, the objective is to get those listening to buy or buy-in to the ideas being delivered. The method of delivery is some sort of formal narrative performed for the benefit of other human beings. Some will have slides, some will rely solely on the words of the speaker. Some will be delivered by individuals, some by a team. Some will happen in-person, some down the lens of the camera. All, unwittingly, have their roots in the oratorical traditions of the ancient Greeks (but that's a whole other book!).

Pitches and presentations aren't new. They aren't simple either. In a desperate attempt to get things right we can tie ourselves up in knots and deliver a performance that is disappointingly underwhelming or even worse, damaging to our prospects.

Over the years, I've watched well-intentioned people fall short of the impact they hoped for: charismatic presenters who missed the mark through over-reliance on charm; teams who, on paper, were favourites to win huge deals but failed to connect with their pitch-day audience; leaders who couldn't energize their people; and speakers who left conference halls yawning – all because their content and delivery lacked the vital ingredients that create cut-through.

Step back for a moment and you'll see that – like so much in life – crafting and delivering a world-class pitch or presentation follows a natural, repeatable process. Just as a tree must flower before it can produce fruit, you must complete every stage if you want to achieve your goal.

We live in a time-poor world where we're always looking for a shortcut. If that's what you were hoping for when you picked up this book, I'd encourage you to stop reading now.

That's not to say that reading these pages can't save you time in the long run and that there won't be plenty of quick wins along the way. However, if you are hoping there's a method for delivering something memorable without putting in some hard work behind the scenes, I'm likely to disappoint you.

As you get more familiar and proficient in working through the six Ds, the six essential steps I'm about to share, you'll inevitably speed up. With dedication and practice, elements of the process will become unconscious and won't need time formally allocating to them. But in order to go fast we must first go slow. Each step is important and can't be rushed. Let's look at each of them in turn.

Step 1: Discover

The first step is to understand the big picture. Too often on being asked to prepare a presentation or to respond to an RFP (Request for Proposal) people start immediately compiling content. Instead, the first step should be a step back. What's being asked of you? Who will be in the audience? What is unique about your ideas or response? There are so many questions that need to be answered before you give any thought to structuring your narrative.

Step 2: Distil

Once you've done that all-important thinking, the next step is to distil your ideas. It's all about getting specific. Given what you've discovered, what should your key messages be? What should you include and – more importantly – what can you leave out? What is the emotional journey you want to take your audience on? What examples and case studies do you have to help you reinforce your points? Making these decisions early will save you time later.

Step 3: Design

This is the first time in the process you need to start thinking about what it looks like and how it will be delivered. Up until this point it's all been about gathering and refining your ideas. Now your attention can turn to how you package it all up. How will you structure things? Will you use slides? How do you make it flow? What is missing or needs reinforcing? After all the hard work in the early steps, the shape and form of the presentation emerges, ready to be spoken into life.

Step 4: Drill

The fourth step is often the scariest. It's the one I see clients trying their hardest to avoid. And yet it's where you find out what works and what doesn't. Rehearsal is a vital part of the process. By drilling your performance, you discover where the gaps are. Nothing is set in stone. Preparing for all eventualities gives you the greatest chance of being at your best when the time to deliver comes.

Step 5: Deliver

From how you warm up, to how you handle objections, there are multiple variables at play when you're pitching and presenting in front of an audience. Knowing where to place your focus and how to make people want to listen is vital. And if those difficult questions come, and they inevitably will, having tools in your tool kit to help you answer them with confidence ensures you'll be remembered for the right reasons. Most of the time you only get the chance to pitch or present once. You need to make it count.

Step 6: Debrief

Logging out of the meeting or walking out of the door isn't the end of the process. An important step that is often overlooked is the debrief. What lessons can you take away? What would you do differently if given the chance again? Elite athletes get taught to analyze their performance at a granular level and learn from their failure and their success. The more open we are to feedback and the more able we are to objectively critique our delivery, the quicker our skills will grow.

Discover, Distil, Design, Drill, Deliver and Debrief. Following these six steps will maximize your chance of success in any pitch or presentation. In the chapters that follow I'll dig into each in detail and walk you through practical, actionable techniques that you can use immediately. We need to move away from theory and toward action.

If you're ready to roll your sleeves up and do the work, let's start by understanding your current performance.

Figure 2 Six Ds

Benchmark your performance

Warren Buffett is supposed to have said 'If you can't read the scoreboard, you don't know the score. If you don't know the score, you can't tell the winners from the losers'. In the world of pitches and presentations we're only really competing against ourselves. As much as we try, we can't fully control how our audience reacts. We can only take responsibility for our own performance. If we can, hand on heart, say we did our best in all the areas under our control, we can walk away with our head held high, no matter the outcome.

Given that we are our own biggest competitor, it's useful to have a way to benchmark what we're doing. We need to see where the gaps lie and to chart the progress we are making in any given area. To help you do that I've created *The Cut-Through Scorecard*. It's made up of a series of questions and will give you a score in each of the six Ds. Before you read on, I'd recommend you take five minutes to answer them and discover where your strengths and weaknesses lie.

Your personalized report will provide suggestions for where you should place your focus, so that as you read the chapters that follow, you'll have a clearer idea about which of the tools and techniques you need to prioritize. You can also re-take the assessment in the future to track your progress and improve your performance.

• •

 To complete the scorecard and receive your personalized report, visit www.cut-throughbook. com/scorecard.

• •

Stand and deliver

Now you know you've got a baseline (if you haven't completed *The Cut-Through Scorecard* go back and do it now!) it's time to do the work. I'd recommend you go through this playbook systematically.

Don't try to change everything at once. Take it one step at a time. Test the ideas I'm about to share in the real world, get feedback and chart your progress.

Remember that actions speak louder than words. Reading a book on pitching and presentation skills might be thought provoking but if you don't take action, it all remains theoretical. Data for later. The only way you'll grow your skills and improve is if you do something.

To give you the best possible chance of doing that, I've scattered 'Stand and deliver' activities throughout the text. Just look out for this icon:

These sections contain practical exercises and suggestions that will supercharge your implementation of the ideas contained within these pages. Rather than adding them to your to-do list and continuing to read, I suggest pausing at each of these junctures and following the instructions I have laid out.

Each 'Stand and deliver' activity will help you embed the tools and techniques into your toolkit and offer strategies for making them your own. Taking time to complete them will ensure that you start to build your skillset in each of the six Ds and will deepen your understanding of the concepts and ideas I am sharing.

When you see a presenter who looks effortless, it's because they have put in the reps to refine their craft. What was once conscious behaviour has become unconscious. They have created a muscle memory and the performance flows.

If you've read this far, I know you're serious about developing your ability to create cut-through. Don't sell yourself short and skip the opportunity to achieve mastery. It will take you longer to get to the end of the book, but the experience will be richer and the learning will be deeper as a result.

Now that you're fully committed, let's take the first step.

Chapter one

DISCOVER: Zoom out to the big picture

Step 1: Discover

The first step in this playbook is DISCOVER. In the time-poor world we live in most of us want to spring into action. We open a new file (or worse copy an old one!) and crack on with creating our content. Unfortunately, this approach is flawed. It leads to generalized messaging, forgettable content and often a disengaged audience. If you want to increase your chances of success, before you start putting metaphorical pen to paper, there is some deep thinking you need to do first. You need to lay the foundations for success and that requires you to take a step back.

As an actor and director, I noticed that my experience in the rehearsal room was directly correlated to the quality of the final performance. If rehearsals went well, you could be relatively confident that the audience would enjoy the show. If rehearsal went badly, then you were in for a bumpy ride. However, not all parts of the rehearsal process were created equal. The most enjoyable and successful shows I worked on had one thing in common: rehearsals that started with research and discussion not jumping straight to your feet.

Working with corporate clients today, the same thing is true. Whether it's leaders giving speeches at conferences or business development teams pitching for new opportunities, those that are most successful in their endeavours are those that take time up front for research, discussion and preparation. The result is content and messaging that is more tailored and relevant, which in turn creates much higher audience engagement, ultimately leading to a higher likelihood of the pitch or presentation achieving the desired outcome.

Spending time in the DISCOVER phase pays dividends later. Let's look at the sort of things you should consider.

Don't be afraid to say no

In life what you say 'no' to is just as important (if not more so) than what you say 'yes' to. The same is true with pitches and presentations. Sometimes opting out is much more sensible than opting in. A well designed and delivered presentation takes time and effort. Before you embark on the process of creation you need to ensure there will be a return on investment.

Not all prospects are a good fit for what you offer. Not all topics are within your area of expertise. Not all questions require an answer. Before you wade in and start preparing, I'd encourage you to pause and take a deep breath.

In a sales context what's the likelihood of converting this opportunity? If this is an internal presentation to your team or your boss, are you the right person for the task? Is there another more impactful way the information could be delivered? A video? A document? A more informal conversation? Crafting a great pitch or presentation requires you to invest yourself in the process. You need to ask yourself if the juice is worth the squeeze.

Sometimes it feels like we don't have a choice. Someone more senior has asked us to do it. We've been told that it's part of the job. But that doesn't mean we need to run headfirst into the task without taking time to think. When we say 'yes' to anything, by definition we are saying 'no' to something else. We need to be aware of the opportunity cost. We need to be strategic in our decision making.

The first step is really understanding what I like to call the 'exam question'. I know the E-word fills some people with dread, but we must understand the question we are answering for our audience. Defining it as an 'exam question' helps us understand the stakes. There's an A* outcome and an F outcome and a plethora of shades in-between.

There are of course lots of different 'exam questions' you could be facing: 'What's the best approach for the team to take on project X?', 'How does your product solve problem Y for the prospect?', 'Why are you best suited to job role Z?'. Your job is to ensure the question is clearly defined and you understand it well.

Get good at asking questions rather than assuming that you know what your audience wants. Different stakeholder may have different expectations too, so you need to clarify these with the person or people you will be presenting to before you decide on how to proceed.

No one wants to fail. So how do you increase your chance of success?

When you stop to think about the question your presentation is meant to answer, if you're not confident of achieving at least a metaphorical B grade I would counsel you against proceeding. You don't want to become memorable for all the wrong reasons. Instead look at the other options available to you. Could you bring in a co-presenter? Could you deliver the material in a different way? And slightly more extreme (but equally as valid), especially in a sales context, if it's not a good fit can you walk away?

If you're confident of your chances of success and you understand what is being asked it's time to switch your focus.

Know your audience

It's not about you. It never has been and never will be.

Despite the fact that you might be the one speaking, that you might be the one sharing your data or your ideas, you're always the least important person in the room or on the video call. We need to get clear on that upfront, otherwise we'll limit your chances of success.

Whenever we communicate, and even more importantly in pitches and presentations, our primary focus should always be our audience. It doesn't matter how good your ideas are, if you can't bring them to life in the hearts and minds of the people you're talking to, they stand for nothing.

The problem is most of the time your audience doesn't speak your language. I'm not talking about conversing in a foreign tongue. I'm talking about delivering your message in a way that resonates deeply with the people you're in front of. Too often I see people making massive assumptions about their audience's understanding of a topic. They speak about themselves and their own perspective, expecting that to excite those listening.

People don't care about you, your idea, your product or service. They only really care about what you, your idea, your product or service can do for them. I'm being a little bit hard of course. I'm sure most people care about you a little bit. But the biggest question in your audience's mind is always 'what's in it for me'?

When we think about pitches and presentations that poses a bit of a challenge. It means you can't roll out the same tried and tested material for every single audience. It also means if your audience consists of more than one person, you can't take a one-size-fits-all approach, you've got to think about how you can give everyone a little bit of something that appeals directly to them. Before we get into how to do that, let's think a little bit more deeply about who's in front of us in the first place.

Several years ago, I was directing a production of Hamlet for Cunard's QM2 cruise ship. That's a very specific audience. Traditional. Conservative. At the same time as my production was sailing the seven seas, one of my favourite actors, Michael Sheen, was giving his Hamlet in a Young Vic production in London. The two shows couldn't have been more different. The Young Vic's was edgy, ours was much more classical. Yet both were getting standing ovations. If we'd put my show in front of the London audience, it would have flopped. If we'd put the Young Vic production on the QM2, audiences would have walked out. The words – the scripts – were exactly the same but how it was packaged and delivered to the audience was completely different.

That packaging took a lot of thought. The creative team and I made strategic choices about how we should put the show together. From how I edited the script, to the actors that we cast, the set we built, the costumes we made, the lighting we used and the soundscape we created, every choice started with the audience in mind. Luckily, I had directed shows onboard before, so I had first-hand experience, but we also did our research to understand the demographic we were trying to appeal to.

If we bring things back into the business world there are numerous ways you can approach that research. I'd encourage you to be vigorous. Time spent understanding who you're talking to upfront will pay off later on. The great thing about the age we live in is that information abounds. A quick internet search will normally bring up numerous results on the people you'll be speaking to and if you're presenting internally many organizations have staff databases with profiles for each employee.

Don't limit yourself on the type of information that you're searching for. Job titles and career history are all very well and can normally be found on social media profiles, especially LinkedIn. More useful though is to read between the lines and look out for more personal information. Does the person support a certain charity? Do they have a particular interest in sport? Have they commented on a post from someone else that might give you some insight into the way they see the world? I'm not for a second suggesting cyber-stalking but I would encourage you to be a detective and find out as much as possible.

Another thing I always do is search for videos of the person speaking. Many key decision makers have spoken at conferences or appeared on podcasts. Being able to see them speak before you meet for the first time is really useful. It gives you a feel for who you're going to encounter, lets you hear their tone of voice and can also provide useful insight into their way of thinking.

Don't forget to speak to other people too. Desk-based research is great but given our digital connectedness I estimate we're now even less than 'six degrees of separation' from anyone on the planet. Reach out to your network. Speak to your colleagues. Find out as much as you possibly can about what makes your audience tick so that you can then start to go about tailoring your approach.

It may sound obvious, but you can also speak directly to your prospective audience too. In a sales context ask for a pre-call with the key decision makers and find out what's important to them. If you're speaking at a conference request access to two or three delegates ahead of your presentation and find out what they're hoping for from your session. People love to be asked their views, and it gives you a great opportunity to build rapport before you deliver the real thing.

If you're looking for your audience to make a decision after your presentation, speaking to them directly in advance also gives you an opportunity to discover who the key decision makers are, who influences them and whether there are any advocates or detractors you should be aware of.

As you start to dig deeper, you'll uncover all sorts of information but do be careful. Not all information is created equal. Some of what you find will be *facts*. Empirical evidence that would stand up in a court of law. Where the person has worked. Where they went to school. What good causes they support. What their hobbies are. These *facts* can help you tailor your message so that you speak your audience's language.

There is, however, another category of information that can be really useful but comes with a health warning. That category is *feelings*. This type of information often comes to us second hand; 'they're not bought into the project', 'they've already made up their mind'. We can also make it up ourselves 'they don't like me', or 'they were bored in our last meeting'. We shouldn't dismiss *feelings* out of hand. They can help us consider our audience from 360 degrees. However, we need to test their validity and be prepared to challenge them. People change, situations evolve, so do your research but always meet your audience in the present moment and be prepared to be surprised.

A great tool to help you stay flexible is to start by putting people in boxes.

STAND & DELIVER

FACTS VS FEELINGS

Think about your next audience. Grab a piece of paper or open up a document. Write the name of each person down the right-hand side leaving space for notes between each name. If you don't have the person's name, write down their job title or a description (then make it's your number one priority to find out!).

If you're presenting to a more unknown audience, for example at a conference, you can still do this exercise by generalizing they types of people who might be in the room e.g., business owners, salespeople, accountants, etc. Create an 'avatar' for each audience segment.

Now you have your list, write at least five things that you know about each person. Ideally aim for ten. These don't have to be earth shattering: job title, tenure at the company, hobbies, interests, number of children, level of excitement about the topic you'll be presenting, likelihood to say yes, etc. Think as broadly as you can.

Now grab two highlighters or use the highlighter function on your device to categorize each thing. Use one colour for *facts* – things that are empirically true, and another for *feelings* – things that may or not be true and are open to interpretation. Spend a minute or two reviewing the colour-coded list. What does it tell you about the person or people in your audience? How do you need to tailor your content or approach accordingly? How can you use the *facts* to build connection and rapport? Do the *feelings* help or hinder you? Can you discount them, or do you need to address them?

Put people in boxes

No one likes to be pigeonholed. I'm a fully signed-up believer that every human being is unique. However, that doesn't mean that generalization doesn't come in handy. What if there were some shortcuts for understanding your audience's preferences and helping you to speak their language?

Back when I was training to be an actor, we spent a lot of time focusing on the psychological makeup of the characters we were portraying. We had a regular class called Movement Psychology which was taught by an inspiring man called Yat Malmgren. Yat, who was in his 80s when he taught me, had been a world-famous soloist dancer. When he retired from the stage, he teamed up with the psychologist William Carpenter to help actors bring their characters to life by combining thought and movement. I could write a whole other book about Yat's approach but what's most fascinating to me now is how strongly it applies to real-life communication and not just characters on stage and screen.

Most people have come across psychological profiling tools at some point in their career. There is a plethora to choose from and most have an underlying basis in Jungian archetype. Yat's work did too. So, when I started working with businesses, I got curious about the overlap and started looking for the hidden pattern. What I discovered was that Yat's approach focused on four types of energy, four areas of the body that people communicate from.

Over the last ten years I've tested this concept with thousands of delegates and refined the methodology. I call them the *In Flow Energy Centres*:

- The head
- The heart
- The gut
- The feet

Of course, as well-rounded human beings, we communicate with a mixture of all four energies but if we look carefully, we can usually discover what someone's preference is, or which centre is currently dominating their communication. Once we spot this, if we're flexible, we can adjust our own style so that we are talking in a way that speaks directly to them.

In my first book, *IMPACT*, I explored the *In Flow Energy Centres* from a more general communication perspective. Here I'd like to look at them through the lens of pitches and presentations. How can you identify which centre someone is communicating from, or what their preferred energy centre is? And how do you flex your approach to resonate with them more? Let's look at each energy in turn.

Head energy

This is the energy of logic. Head people want to understand the detail, in detail. They won't put up with the fluffy and opaque, they want clarity and concrete evidence. 'What are the numbers?', 'How did you reach this conclusion?', 'What other options or ideas have you looked at?'. You can start to recognize this energy centre from the type and quantity of questions you are asked. If someone is getting into minutiae, they're bringing head energy to the table.

When you're pitching to this type of person or audience it's all about the structure and the logic. You need to be precise, considered and factual. You need to appeal to their intellect and help them gain a crystal-clear understanding of your ideas. If things don't make sense, you can easily end up down a rabbit hole, having to give explanations and justifications. It's not necessarily about producing tons of slides, or spreadsheets galore, but when you get into the DESIGN phase you might want to create an appendix of information that you can call on should the need arise.

Head people are often reflectors too and take time to process any information you share with them. If you're looking for a decision, try to ensure that they're not seeing or hearing the information you're sharing for the first time. You'll be much more successful if you can share documentation with them in advance so that they arrive at your pitch or presentation ready to ask questions and take action.

Heart energy

This is the energy of compassion. Heart people will always put people over profit. They want to create consensus, make sure all voices are heard, and all stakeholders are involved. 'How will this impact the team?', 'What is the underlying purpose?', 'Who will be involved?'. People with this energy centre will often talk about how things feel and use 'we' and 'us' statements rather than 'I' and 'me' statements. They're unlikely to be pushy and will switch off very quickly if they feel they are being 'lectured to' rather than being involved in a conversation.

If you want to get a heart audience excited about your presentation, you have to paint the big picture. They need to understand the purpose behind your ideas or proposal. It's not all about the bottom line for this type of person, you must be able to articulate what your proposal means for individuals, teams, the wider organization or society as a whole.

Heart people really value being heard and having the time and space to articulate their emotions. If you can't get them to emotionally connect to what you're talking about they're unlikely to act. With this type of audience, it pays to ask them questions rather than expecting them to ask you. Ask them how they're feeling about what's being discussed and then really listen to their response. Taking time to build relationships and understand their perspective will pay dividends.

Gut energy

This is the energy of creation. Gut people love to engage and try new things. They're not interested in getting bogged down in the detail and gravitate towards options and opportunity. 'What's the story you're trying to tell?', 'What's next after this?', 'What else can you offer?'. A gut audience will generally bring a lot of energy to the conversation and want to have a dialogue. They'll be open and receptive to new ideas but can switch off quickly if things become too technical or prescriptive.

The key to presenting to this type of audience is keeping things dynamic. You can't expect them to be excited about your ideas if you're not excited too. Storytelling is a powerful tool for engaging gut people. Paint them a picture of what success looks like and help them understand their role in the journey. Tap into their natural preference for optimism and steer clear of too much detail unless they explicitly ask for it.

It's worth bearing in mind that gut people can sometimes be difficult to contain and can easily unintentionally hijack a conversation. You need to tread the line between involving them and not letting them dominate. With their love of new ideas and exciting possibilities you'll benefit from setting clear ground rules for how you want to structure your presentation. If you want it to be a flowing conversation that's fine but if you'd like to walk through your ideas and then open things up for questions, make sure you agree that up front.

Feet energy

This is the energy of action. Feet people have their eyes firmly fixed on the prize. They're all about outcomes and results, constantly taking steps towards their goal. The journey is less important to this type of audience, it's reaching the destination that counts. 'What's the ROI on this?', 'What's the timeline we're looking at?', 'How much will it cost?'. You can expect a feet audience to be direct and to the point. They're likely to interrupt if they don't understand something and to switch off quickly if they don't see the value you are bringing to the table.

If you want buy-in from this type of audience and don't want them to walk away, you need to be able to articulate your ideas clearly and concisely. Time is of the essence. The quicker you can get to the point the better. Feet people aren't afraid to ask for more detail if they need it but as general rule less is more. Keep your narrative outcome focused and be ready to back your ideas up with facts and a clear plan. Decisiveness and confidence win in this type of environment so make sure you've done your homework.

If feet energy isn't your own default style, it's a common misconception to see this type of energy as aggressive or rude. In fact, when you learn to flex into this more direct way of communicating it can be incredibly liberating. This is an energy that drives action and accountability. It doesn't mean you can't build personal relationships with feet people, or get them to engage with the detail or the story, but if you want to talk their language, those things come later.

Table 1 provides a useful overview of the *In Flow Energy Centres*, the characteristics you can expect, the attitude you might encounter and the language you might hear.

The key to using the *In Flow Energy Centres* is flexibility. You need to react to what is happening in the moment. You may do your research and decide that all the members of the group you are presenting to tend to default to 'feet energy'. However, as the conversation progresses, if you start getting lots of questions about the detail and requests for facts and figures, you need to be prepared to drop your plan and start engaging with the 'head energy' in the room. The more flexible you are, the more effective you will be.

When faced with a large audience or when, despite your best efforts, you can't find out a great deal about the people you'll be talking to, the best tactic is to hedge your bets. Often when I'm speaking at conferences the audiences are from a range of backgrounds and job roles. In those instances, my approach is to make sure I plan a little something for everyone:

> ▶ Some clear, actionable, takeaways for the feet people

> ▶ Some well researched data for the head people

- Plenty of human connection for the heart people
- Some energy and storytelling for the gut people

You need to provide everyone with a little bit of something that speaks directly to them. When you do, you'll create more cut-through and reap the rewards.

Table 1 The In Flow Energy Centres

HEAD	FEET
Characteristics	**Characteristics**
Analytical. Detail focused. Logical. Precise. Consistent. Structured.	Driven. Outcome focused. Competitive. Persistent. Strong-willed. Fast paced.
Attitude	**Attitude**
Show me the detail.	Show me the outcome.
Language	**Language**
• The evidence suggests that…	• Our recommendation is…
• The best process is…	• The time for action is now…
• How do we know this?	• Will it move us towards our goal?
HEART	GUT
Characteristics	**Characteristics**
Caring. Relationship focused. Supportive. Trusting. Reliable. Patient.	Impulsive. Options focused. Sociable. Dynamic. Optimistic. Enthusiastic.
Attitude	**Attitude**
Show me the impact.	Show me the options.
Language	**Language**
• It feels like…	• There are several possibilities…
• The consequences will be…	• The exciting thing is…
• How will this affect others?	• Is there another way?

Now you've deeply understood your audience, it's finally time to think about what you want.

· ·

 To download a free copy of the In Flow Energy Centres cheat sheet visit www.cut-throughbook.com.

· ·

 STAND & DELIVER

· ·

WHO AM I TALKING TO?

One of the most powerful things you can do to help yourself prepare for a pitch or presentation is to map the audience. Take a blank piece of paper or open a new word-processing document and divide the page into four. Label the top left, 'Head', the top right 'Feet', the bottom left 'Heart' and the bottom right 'Gut'. Now start to mentally work through your audience and write each person's name into the box you think best describes their energy. If you're struggling, you can write their name across the dividing lines but ideally each person should be assigned a primary *In Flow Energy Centre*.

Look at the 'audience map' you've created. Which *In Flow Energy Centre* do you tend to default to? How can you flex your approach to speak to those who sit in the other three boxes? How do you need to tailor the information you are presenting to make sure it lands? Keep coming back to this audience map as you create your presentation to make sure your approach will keep everyone engaged.

· ·

Know what you want

When I was training to be an actor there was one question that was asked of me more than any other: What do you want? This question was used to interrogate the character's motivation in a scene but it's just as useful when applied in a communication context.

Obvious right? But my experience working with tens of thousands of people over the last decade suggests that whilst it's a simple question, it's not always an easy one to answer. Unless we can pinpoint exactly what we're looking to achieve, how can we ever know if we have hit the target?

What's required is a clarity of focus. We have to be able to clearly articulate for ourselves what success looks like. Is it sign-off from our boss? Is it agreement from our co-workers? Is it a signature on the contract? Or is it just getting to the end without stumbling over our words and looking silly? What is our goal?

Don't fall into the trap of assuming that what you want is obvious. Taking a little bit of time at this stage will avoid a whole world of pain later on. You don't want to discover three weeks down the line that all the preparation you've been doing doesn't actually move your audience to where you want them to go.

Too often the outcome we are picturing is too wishy-washy, too vague to be useful. So how do we sharpen it up? How do we bring it into focus? The trick is to visualize the moment of success and the path towards it. In the sports world, visualization is a completely normal part of the preparation process but in the average workplace it often gets left out.

When I interviewed four-time World Champion kayaker Anna Hemmings for my *Why Life's A Pitch* podcast, she was clear on the importance of visualization in her race preparation: 'You can't achieve what you can't see, what you can't imagine. When I've seen it, I then start to believe that this can happen.'[1] It's a process that's helped Anna achieve gold on multiple occasions. But what is it that we need to be visualizing?

The most important aspect to be able to picture is the moment just after you achieve your goal. How do you know that you've done it? What reaction will you get from the audience? Whose faces will you see? What words will be said? What specific actions will take place? A shake of hands? A tumultuous round of applause? A standing ovation?

Once you're able to picture the outcome, once you can *see* it, the next step is to *feel* it. What emotion will you experience in that moment? Will it be filled with relief, excitement or contentment? Or even a mixture of all three? Other emotions are available of course but if you can start to imagine how you would feel when you achieve the thing you want to achieve, you're one step closer to achieving it.

The human brain has very little ability to distinguish between what is real and what is imagined. If you can help it produce the chemical cocktail of hormones and neurotransmitters that create the emotions of success, you start to wire the brain to take you there. The more specific you are about the feeling, the easier it will be to determine whether or not you achieved it when the time comes to perform.

The final step, once you can *see* it and *feel* it, is to *say* it. Most people's instinct is to try to articulate the outcome first, but I'd encourage you to follow this more embodied process. Once you've built a clear visual and emotional representation of the moment of success, it should be much easier to put it into words. At this stage the key is to be as specific as possible.

Avoid generalizations and making the goal too big. Is the objective of the pitch really to get them to say yes? Or is to get them to agree to the next meeting? Or to bring someone else into the conversation? If what you want is a follow up call rather than sign off on a $1million budget, your approach to the process of crafting and delivering your presentation will be very different. I'm not suggesting you take your eye off the ultimate prize, but you need to be incredibly particular about what you want in that moment.

Get good at distilling your goal down into as few words as possible. Three to five is awesome but always challenge yourself to make sure it's fewer than ten. There's a reason that bumper stickers have cut-through!

Once you've clearly defined your goal, it's time to put together the team that's going to help you achieve it.

 STAND & DELIVER

● ●

SEE IT. FEEL IT. SAY IT.

Getting crystal clear on your goal early in the DISCOVER phase will save you time and effort later. Before you put pen to paper or start creating a slide deck, take time to sit quietly. Get comfortable. Ideally close your eyes. Think about the task at hand and start to picture the moment just after you achieve your goal. What does it look like? Who's there? What are they saying or doing? Be as specific as possible. Try to create an HD movie in your mind.

Once you can *see* it, you need to *feel* it. Add in the emotion. Don't just intellectualize it, try to experience it in your body. If you'd expect to feel joy allow yourself to feel joyful as you play the movie over and over in your mind. Imagine the emotion on a scale of one to ten where one is low and ten is high. Your job is to turn that emotion up to a level ten. You need to create a connection between how you *see* it and how you *feel* it.

Only when you've got a vivid picture and feeling of success in mind, is it time to commit things to words and *say* it. Your aim here is to distil what you want down into its simplest form. Five to ten words is a good rule of thumb. If someone asked you the question 'What do you want?' how would you answer it with clarity and simplicity? Say the words aloud. No, really, say the words aloud. You need to experience them coming out of your mouth. Can you speak the words with conviction? Do they feel authentic? If not, keep working on them until they do. Once you're happy, write this goal statement on a sticky note and have it with you whenever you're working on the project. It will keep you focused on the right outcome!

• •

Pick the right team

There's no doubt that pitching or presenting solo is simpler than co-presenting. You don't need to schedule time in people's diaries for rehearsal, you don't need to incorporate varying perspectives or approaches, and you don't need to worry about the team dynamic. If the option of incorporating others into your performance isn't available to you feel free to skip this section but if you just hadn't considered it, I'd encourage you to read on.

We can't be expert in everything, and we won't automatically gel with every audience we find ourselves in front of, so, especially when the stakes are high, it's worth considering who else should be on your team. Co-presenting is also a great way of sharing the pressure and responsibility of the moment, so if being in the spotlight doesn't come naturally to you, I'd recommend exploring who else could support you as well.

Who could help you shine? Whose expertise and experience would it be useful to showcase? Who could help you better answer some of the inevitable questions that will come up?

Like any high-performing team, the dynamic is really important. No matter how talented, a group of individuals all pulling in different directions and fighting for the limelight is likely to alienate the audience. Creating coherence is paramount.

It's also worth paying attention to team size. A great presentation is like a well-rehearsed stage play. Every player should have their part. It's fine to have certain people taking the lead but someone lurking in the background, not actively participating becomes a distraction. The audience will wonder why they're there and if they eventually come to speak, they'll lack credibility. Everyone needs a voice. When the time comes to put everything together, make sure you bear that in mind.

You also need to be aware of your audience. Having more speakers than listeners creates a strange dynamic, so aim to make your team smaller than the audience. In my experience a maximum of four people is a good rule of thumb. Larger than that is still possible, but your choreography and timing have to be incredibly refined to pull it off.

When deciding who should present think about the following ABC:

- Approach
- Background
- Credentials

Approach

Approach is about balancing styles and energy. The *In Flow Energy Centres* we covered earlier are a good place to start. Does everyone on the team have the same presenting style or is there a nice mix? Can someone clearly articulate the story (gut energy), whilst someone else can gets into the detail if necessary (head energy)? Do you have someone who's direct and succinct (feet energy) or someone who can connect emotionally (heart energy)? It's often useful to have a balance of introverts and extroverts too. A big bold, expressive presentation style is great but it's also useful to be able to switch energy to something more considered and conversational. Awareness is the key. The team members' approaches need to be complimentary and not work against each other, otherwise you'll fail to put the audience at ease.

Background

Background is also worth taking into consideration. Do you have diversity within the team? Not just from an age, ethnicity or gender perspective but also in terms of diversity of thinking. If you can, it's good to build a presentation team that has similarities to the audience. As human beings we tend to feel more comfortable with similarity, as it normally equates with a reduction in threat. Unconsciously we rationalize that if the people in front of us are like us, they're less likely to pose any danger. Building a pitch team in this way can be a real advantage, especially in a sales context.

Credentials

Credentials is the final category to consider. What expertise and experience do you have to choose from? Again, the more relevant the team's experience and knowledge base is to the audience, the more receptive the audience are likely to be to the message. Make sure you spend time thinking about how what you've done in the past is relevant to those you will be speaking to. It will help you craft a much more compelling message.

No matter how the team is made up, the most important thing is having clearly defined roles. I'd counsel against a flat team structure in this context. It's much more effective to have a clear leader. That doesn't mean that they should take all the airtime, but it does mean that someone has ultimate responsibility for how the pitch or presentation is put together and delivered. It also means that when you finally get in front of your audience someone is responsible for conducting the flow, fielding questions and making sure that the key messages and calls to action are delivered.

Once you've decided whether you're going it alone or assembling a dream team you next need to uncover what makes you special.

Celebrate your uniqueness

People buy people. A winning pitch or an engaging presentation is about standing out from the crowd. You need to be memorable. That means you must be able to articulate what makes you or your team unique. We'll deal with your key messages or why your product or service is a good fit later. At this stage we need to stay focused on the human element. Why are you the right person or people to be delivering this message? What's special about you? What do you bring to the table that no-one else does or can?

Personally, I used to find this part of the process incredibly uncomfortable. I worried that I'd be seen as bragging or singing my own praises. But if you don't know why people should pay attention to you, it's very unlikely that they will work it out for themselves. It's absolutely essential that you embrace your uniqueness. If you can't clearly articulate why you're the best person to be talking on this topic, maybe someone else should be doing it!

The trick is connecting your story to the audience's need. What is it about you that makes you uniquely placed to share your ideas? Which elements of the team's experience give them credibility in this space? Like most things when you're pitching and presenting, the more specific you can be the better. Generic should be avoided at all costs. If someone else could give the same reason you don't have cut-through.

This is not a time for subtlety and modesty. You don't have to be brash or boastful, but you mustn't ask your audience to join the dots. You have to do it for them. 'I've spent the last five years working in the industry'. Generic and forgettable. 'I've spent the last five years working in the industry, with a portfolio of clients very similar to you. Six months ago, one of them was facing the same challenge as you are, and I helped them to successfully navigate it'. Much more tailored and compelling. Often the standout piece of information is hiding in plain sight, you just need to be brave enough to share it.

Once you know what makes you unique, you need to make sure you build it into your narrative. It's not just something to put into the introduction and hope for the best. It's a key piece of information that needs to be continuously and subtlety reinforced. If you asked the audience at the end of the presentation what they thought made you different or most qualified to talk about the topic, would they give the same answer?

If you're reading these words thinking this all feels like an act of self-promotion, I'd encourage you to reframe it as an act of generosity. When you're clear on why your audience should be listening to you and you're able to humbly communicate that to them, they can stop worrying that they're in the wrong room and start listening to what you have to say.

Now you've got your own story sorted, it's time to pay more attention to the competition.

There's always competition

It's rarely a one-horse race. In his brilliant book, *To Sell is Human*, Dan Pink says something worth paying attention to whatever your job title: 'The existing data show that 1 in 9 Americans works in sales. But the new data reveals something more startling: So do the other 8 in 9. They, too, are spending their days moving others and depending for their livelihoods on the ability to do it well.'[2]

Pitches are obviously an act of selling but even if you're 'just' presenting an idea to your boss or your colleagues I'd challenge you to consider this as an act of selling too. You're asking for their attention and trying to move their thinking. If we accept this premise, the logic follows that something else is true. There is always going to be competition.

Especially when you're presenting internally, it's all too easy to bury your head in the sand and focus on your own message without giving a second thought to your competitors. But we must face facts. Competition comes in all shapes and sizes.

If you're pitching a product or a service, then it's normally pretty obvious who else your audience might be considering or talking to. But when you're delivering a non-sales presentation, it can be a bit hazier. If you're making an ask from your boss, what other asks are your colleagues making at the same moment? If you're presenting at a conference what else is happening during your time slot? If you're presenting in a meeting, what other messages and emails are landing in people's inboxes whilst you're talking?

The first step is to define the competition. It's important to ask not just *who* else you are competing with but *what* else you are competing with? This helps you to grow your awareness and your understanding of your audience. If you can anticipate what is pulling their focus, you can start to work out how to ensure that you are more compelling than the other distractions.

What will the competition be saying about you? What do they offer that you can't? What are some of the areas of similarity? Where is there overlap? Even if your main competitor for someone's attention is their smart phone, it's still worth doing this thinking.

You then need to work out your own key differentiators. What do you offer that the competition can't? How does the uniqueness you've already identified build into your narrative? How do you and your idea stand out from the crowd?

The final step sounds harsh, but you need to figure out how to destroy the competition in your audience's mind. I'm not suggesting for a second you explicitly talk down other people or things; in fact, I'd go as far as to say that's a really bad idea and is likely to make you sound desperate or defensive. Instead, what you do need to have at your fingertips is all the information that neutralizes the competition's claims or attractiveness and can help your audience stay focused on you and your message.

Define. Differentiate. Destroy. Once you've done that it's time to ask a few more questions.

STAND & DELIVER

• •

DEFINE. DIFFERENTIATE. DESTROY

Before you start planning your message, get clear on your competition so that you can work out the best possible way to position your argument. Grab a piece of paper or open a blank document. You'll want to create three columns for this:

1. At the top of column one write DEFINE.

2. At the top of column two write DIFFERENTIATE.

3. At the top of column three write DESTROY.

In column one, list all the people and/or things that are competing for your audience's attention. Take time to consider all possible angles.

In column two, write all the things that differentiate you from the competition. What will make you stand out in your audience's minds?

Finally in column three, write all the things that could destroy the competition's key attractiveness. How could you build a case against their key arguments?

As you craft your presentation or pitch deck, keep referring back to this document. It will ensure you have done everything in your power to maximize your chances of beating the competition.

• •

Go big to go small

Now you've done some serious thinking about your audience, your objective, your team, your uniqueness and your competition, it's almost time to start crafting your presentation and your message.

But before you reach for the PowerPoint (other slide software is available!), I'd encourage you to pause and open your mind. If you want to be able to distil your message down into exactly the right things to say, you must first become aware of everything you possibly *could* say on the topic. It's time to let your brain run wild.

One of the biggest mistakes I see people making when crafting a pitch or presentation is structuring things too early. When you begin ordering your ideas it becomes difficult to make changes later. Do not start by adding slides and titles to an empty deck. Instead, I would encourage you to stay in the realm of 'divergent thinking'. This is the space of creativity and playfulness.

Start by brainstorming and collecting as many different ideas and perspectives as possible. I love sticky notes but a blank piece of paper or a white board will do. Bring together all the thinking you have done so far so that you have the best possible understanding of the big picture.

Once you've captured your thinking in its entirety, look for patterns and themes. What's jumping out at you? What impact does it have on how you will craft your message? You have to go big to go small. The detail will follow later but at this point in the process you need to see the forest from the trees.

Chapter summary

This first step in the playbook has focused on the big picture. You start by deciding whether the pitch or presentation is the right fit for you and then (assuming it is) your job it to get forensic in your research. Many people find this step frustrating and want to skip over it to the more interesting tasks of crafting their message and rehearsing their performance, but these foundations are essential to your success. Failing to put this work in up front increases the likelihood of problems later. You don't want to be standing up in front of your audience when you discover that you've completely misunderstood them and that you've pitched your message in completely the wrong way. Believe me, I've been there!

Instead, make sure you're crystal clear on the following:

✓ Who is in your audience? Put yourself in their shoes.

✓ What is your goal? See it, feel it, say it.

✓ Who, if anyone, should be on your team? Consider your ABCs.

✓ Why are you uniquely placed to deliver this pitch or presentation? Be generous and create human connection.

✓ Who or what is competing for your audience's attention? Define, differentiate, then destroy.

✓ What are all the possible elements and information that could go into your presentation? Start brainstorming, not creating slides.

Whilst it may feel like a lot, this early reflection and research is where the magic happens. Spend time here up front and you will reduce your time in the later phases and make the whole process smoother. The more consistent you are at doing the work each time you present, the quicker and easier it becomes. If you've skipped any of the earlier sections and can't answer the questions above, go back and do the work. Once you're ready, it's time to strip things back.

Chapter two

DISTIL: Cut it back to the core

Step 2: Distil

You've done the big picture thinking. Now it's time to get specific, which is why Step 2 in this playbook is DISTIL. We're still not at the scripting or collateral creation stage but we do need to start deciding what to keep and what to throw out. By the end of this step, you'll have all the ingredients of a compelling presentation and the recipe for blending them together to create something special. Your job is to be ruthless. When it comes to cut-through less really is more.

Having amassed lots of interesting and relevant information in the DISCOVER phase, I've noticed that lots of people struggle to cut things back. They want to include everything but in doing so they neglect their audience's capacity to process information. Back in 1956, Professor George Miller of Harvard University published a paper entitled *The Magical Number Seven, Plus or Minus Two: Some Limits on our Capacity for Processing Information*.[1] Many people have seized on this research to suggest that humans can process an average of seven chunks of information in their short-term memory. Others have suggested that this is an oversimplification. Regardless of the exact number of bytes or chunks, it's clear, especially in the distracted world we live in, that if we don't make our information easy and logical for our audience to consume, there is a very real risk of losing them.

The best communicators instinctively strip their message back to the bare essentials. As you work on the DISTIL phase of the playbook, your job is to do the same.

Pick the format

If you've engaged fully with the DISCOVER phase, you're probably staring at a huge amount of information that you could possibly include in your pitch or presentation. Your job now is to move from everything you could possibly say about a topic, to what your particular audience needs to hear about this topic, in this particular moment. We need to move from the global to the specific.

Depending on the context this could mean you have some hard choices to make. A useful way to think about things is to decide if you're taking a 'feature film' approach or a 'box set' one. Should you be aiming for a more complex, longer, format that takes us from beginning to end in a single sitting? Or do you need to break your topic up into a series of bite-sized chunks, each equally complete in and of themselves, yet ending on a cliffhanger which leave the audience curious about what is coming in the next instalment?

As attention spans have reduced, so too has the way we consume entertainment. Hollywood A-list celebrities appearing in TV shows was unthinkable 20 years ago. Now it's commonplace. Our appetite for content has shifted from long form to short form and that gives us a good steer for how to think about the presentations we create. TED talks are another great example of this; a life-changing idea, distilled into 18 minutes or less, giving us a complete understanding of the concept the speaker is sharing, whilst at the same time (if done well) leaving us hungry for more.

Traditional sales pitches often require 'feature film' thinking but many presentations, especially internal ones, would really benefit from a 'box set' approach. Plenty of the sales teams I've worked with have adopted the 'box set' method too, creating compelling touch points that move the prospect step by step towards a sale. So much better to leave your audience leaning in and wanting more, than leaning back simultaneously overwhelmed and underwhelmed.

For clarity, you'll rarely be invited to create a 'box set' of presentations, with episode 2, 3, 4, 5 and 6 already scheduled into your audience's diaries. Instead, you have to decide whether or not to take the risk, to package your content is such a way that some stuff inevitably gets left out. When you take this route, your job is to create an experience for your audience that makes sense regardless of whether they see the next instalments. Just like the pilot for a TV show, your presentation must stand on its own without additional context. Do it well and you'll have an audience desperate to find out what's coming next.

Once you're clear on the format, it's time to get to the core of the presentation.

Find the essence

The goal of every great pitch or presentation is to make the audience do something. To produce some sort of action. Whether it's signing a contract, agreeing to a new way of working or supporting a good cause, our words should create momentum. Even in the dullest 'business update' scenario I'd still encourage you to think about what change you're trying to affect. If the presentation really is information for information's sake it might be better just to send an email!

Assuming then that we are aiming for action, we need to get clear on our intention. I devoted an entire chapter of *IMPACT* to this subject because it's so important to get right. When you look at communication in general there are three parts to a well-formed intention:

1. Intellectual

2. Emotional

3. Behavioural

Your intellectual intention is the information you're trying to get across. Your emotional intention is how you want your audience to feel about that information. And your behavioural intention is what you want your audience to do about (or with) the information that you're sharing.

This gives rise to three questions that you always need to be able to answer to plan effectively:

1. What do I want my audience to *know*?

2. What do I want my audience to *feel*?

3. What do I want my audience to *do*?

Answering these three questions gives you a solid base to start building from. However, in a pitch and presentation context I've discovered a fourth question that is vital to your success:

4. Why *now?*

A temporal intention if you like.

Action is at the intersection of logic, emotion and timing. If you're going to persuade your audience to do something, they must understand your argument, have an emotional connection to it and have a sense that now is the time to act.

If one of those three elements is missing nothing happens. Human beings are designed for homeostasis or the status-quo. Change is difficult. If the benefits of doing something differently don't significantly outweigh the drawbacks of keeping things the same, most people are unlikely to make the leap. Helping your audience understand the urgency of your argument becomes essential.

The answers to the four questions above form the essence of our presentation. A filter you can use to decide which elements from the DISCOVER phase make the cut. Every word and every visual

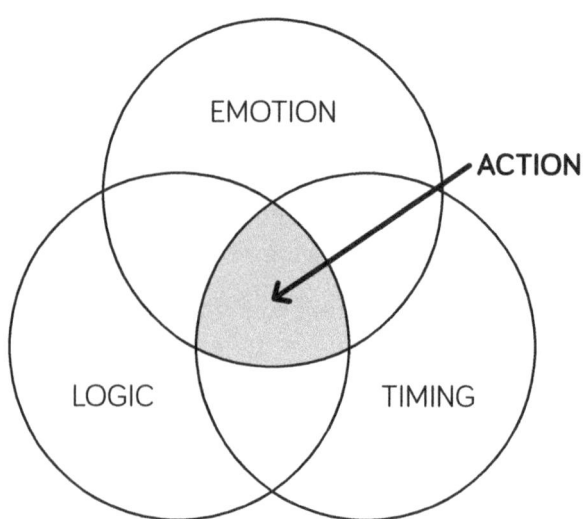

Figure 3 The action sweet spot

that you use should be helping to reinforce these answers. If they don't, you should be very cautious about including them.

To ensure you start from a place of clarity, it's useful to get even more granular.

Write the headline

What sells newspapers isn't great stories, interesting articles or even bad news. What sells newspapers is great headlines. Unless you subscribe and have your favourite rag automatically delivered to your house, what makes you part with your money is the words in bold on the front page. As you walk past the news stand you may be curious. You may even have an allegiance to a particular publication. But if the words in the headline don't jump out and grab you, you're unlikely to part with your hard-earned cash.

In partnership with the cover image chosen by the editor, that small collection of characters on that wafer thin piece of paper, must be compelling enough to stop you in your tracks. Despite the plethora of shiny magazines nearby, the confectionary lining the shelves and the lottery scratch cards on the counter, those words need to hold your attention for enough time for your brain to decide they are of interest and tell your hand to reach out and grab your copy.

A newspaper headline is the ultimate pitch. Broad-sheets tend to use seven to ten words. Tabloids often use three to five words, sometimes fewer. The job of the headline writer is to distil the information contained within the article's pages down into its simplest form. To convert it into a phrase that is 'sticky' and memorable. It's not easy. It takes time and energy. But, done well, it's hugely effective at cutting through the noise.

The most popular YouTubers are brilliant at this too. The video titles they choose are not an accident. They're designed to work alongside the thumbnail image to make it almost irresistible to click, even though there are probably a million other things you should be doing! Next time you're scrolling, notice what catches your eye. What makes the videos you decide to watch stand out from the sea of sameness?

So often, pitches and presentations have sleep-inducing titles like 'Company-wide Q2 Update' or 'ACME Inc's Transformation Proposal for ABC Co'. Tedious and forgettable. But what I'm talking about here is more than an exercise in labelling. This is about uncovering the idea that lies at the heart of your message.

In answer to the question 'what do I want my audience to *know?*', can you reduce your response to a single sentence? If people could know only one thing about your idea, product or service, what would it be? When your audience walk out of the boardroom or log out of the meeting, how would they describe, in a few words, what your presentation was about to someone who wasn't present?

Especially in a business context, it's tempting to play it safe and opt for a broad-sheet style phrase, conservative and factual but not particularly emotive. It is however worth imagining how your message would appear on a more populist publication. A good tabloid headline is usually much more impactful. Whether the aim is to shock, to anger or to titillate, they tend to be much more memorable and evocative than their more predictable, serious counterparts. When the stakes are high there's rarely a prize for second place in someone's memory.

Interestingly once you've discovered the perfect headline, you may end up never using it explicitly. It may feel too salesy or pushy to commit to the page or even to utter aloud. But the act of creating it provides you with a reference point. A way of judging whether your content reinforces or dilutes the idea you are trying to get across. Everything should bring you back to that headline message. You'll need to articulate it in myriad different ways throughout the presentation and constantly make choices that strengthen your argument. But if you've done your job, when the conversation comes to a close, your audience should have your big idea emblazoned in bold letters in their mind.

Now it's time to look at what sits underneath that headline idea.

Harness the power of three

Whilst a headline is designed to grab your attention, on its own it's not enough to hold your focus. In a newspaper context that is done by the subheadings, the phrases in bold that punctuate the body text. For most articles, if you only read the headline and subheadings, you'd have a pretty good idea of what the whole thing was about, without having to consume it word by word. We can borrow this approach when we're thinking about our key messages, the organizing ideas that we are going to build the whole presentation around.

If we're being asked to deliver a message it's normally because we're an expert in the field we're being asked to talk on. In a sales context we know more about our product or service than our customer. In a meeting context we're normally talking about a project that we are involved in. Even if you're still in the process of researching the topic you're going to speak about, you're likely to be at least one step ahead of your audience. That 'expert' status is a blessing and a curse.

I'm not suggesting for a second that it's best to have no idea what you're talking about and make it up on the spot. However, when you have good level of understanding of a particular subject it can make it hard to be objective. What can you leave out? What needs to stay in? So many people cram pitches and presentations full of information. This only serves to overwhelm the audience. It's not their job to decide which parts of your message are important. It's yours! And it's a task that you need to engage with early on.

When you think about everything you could possibility say, what are the most important things that jump out at you? What are the things that, if you only had a minute or two, you'd absolutely want to get across? These are your key messages. I encourage you to get disciplined and boil them down to your top three.

If we go back to Professor Miller's research that I mentioned at the beginning of this chapter, whilst the magic number might be seven, I'm pretty sure that most of us have two or three things sloshing around our short-term memory that we don't want to forget in order to process something new. What are we having for dinner? Or when do we need to pick the kids up from school? It's wise to imagine that our audience are like us too and won't have unlimited bandwidth for our message, no matter how passionate and enthusiastic we may be about sharing it. If that's the case, then I'd like to suggest that, in a presentation context, the magic number is not seven but three.

The power of three is a tried and tested rhetorical device. From Shakespeare's 'Friends, Romans, Countrymen', to Lincoln's 'Life, liberty and the pursuit of happiness', the pattern appeals to the ear and is easy to digest. In his brilliant book, *Winning Minds*, professional speech writer Simon Lancaster make the case for its use: 'Four sounds over-the-top, hyperbolic, exaggerative and a bit bonkers. Two is too little, too measly. Three sounds decisive, complete and final. And critically, it works. Academics have shown that three-part claims are more persuasive than four-part claims.'[2]

When you start looking, you'll notice these triads everywhere. In fact, it was a triad of key messages that Steve Jobs famously used to launch the iPhone, a product that, at the time of writing, has sold more than 2.3 billion units: 'An iPod, a phone and an internet communicator.'[3] What a simple and brilliant pitch! You know exactly what is and what it does in eight words. The rest of the launch event then went on to show you how those three elements combined to create an amazing product.

Having three key messages is a simple idea but it's not always easy to execute. I don't want to be dogmatic so if you honestly believe you have four key messages then you'll probably be fine. At five, I start to question if you're being ruthless enough. Any more than that and you're doing yourself and your audience a disservice. When was the last time you remembered the six key messages someone shared with you in a 30-minute presentation? Find the connections and see how you can group your ideas together to make your presentation simpler and more 'sticky' for your audience.

These key messages become organizing ideas that you can group the rest your information – research, case studies, fact and figures – under. Over the course of an hour-long pitch, you'll share lots of different things but the more you streamline your content to reinforce your key messages, the easier those messages will be to remember. Think of it like a family tree with your headline – the big idea – at the top, your three key messages underneath that, and then all the other stuff – supporting information – sitting underneath each of the key messages.

Busy brains crave logic and order, so the more you can streamline your content and structure it in this way, the easier it is for your audience to consume. It also makes it much easier to plan and develop your material when you have this simple superstructure in place.

Defining these key messages is crucial but your next task is to think about how you bring them to life.

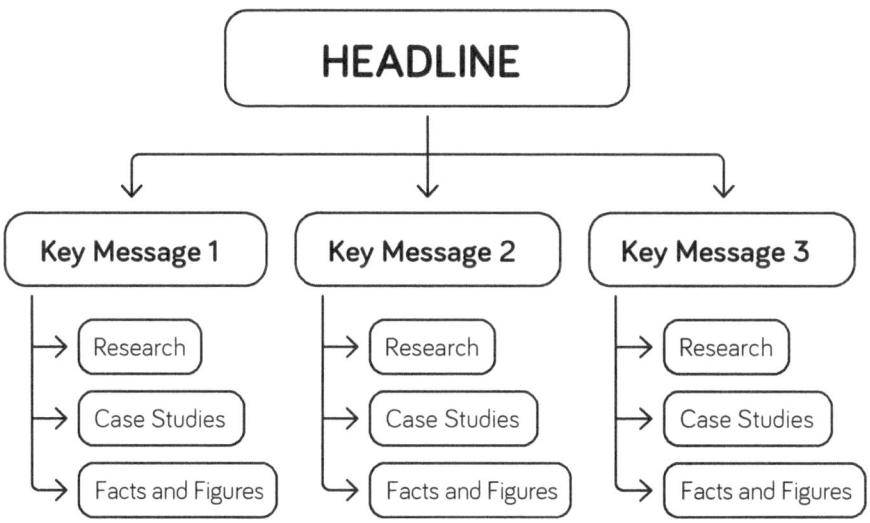

Figure 4 The family tree presentation structure

STAND & DELIVER

· ·

WHAT DO YOU WANT THEM TO *KNOW*?

Getting clear on what you want your audience to *know* – your intellectual intention – is the first step to crafting a compelling pitch or presentation narrative. It's time to narrow down everything you could possibly say to a headline and three to five key messages.

1. Write the headline

If you were going to encapsulate your whole presentation on the front of a newspaper or in the title of a social media video, what words would you use? Keep it short and punchy. Aim for ten words of fewer. This is a phrase you want your audience to remember and be able to share. It doesn't have to be sensationalist but if you can inject some emotion like tabloid newspapers tend to, so much the better.

2. Write down your key messages

What are the key messages that support your headline? What is it essential for your audience to remember? Aim for three sentences, five should be the maximum. Be ruthless. You will use these key messages to structure your presentation.

Let's look at three different examples:

A presentation to a company leadership team by the VP of Sales

Headline:	Revenue targets exceeded by 11%
Key messages:	1. Average order size increased by 6%
	2. 16 new clients won
	3. Pipeline for Q3 healthy

A pitch to an accounting firm by a bookkeeping software company

Headline:	A one-step solution for future-proof bookkeeping
Key messages:	1. AI features double data entry speed
	2. Reduces bookkeeping costs by 25% for the average firm
	3. Integrates with all major accounting software

A presentation to colleague regarding a project update

Headline:	'Project Moonshot' dangerously behind schedule
Key messages:	1. Stage 3 'go live' date missed
	2. Risk assessment still incomplete
	3. Additional budget sign-off required

You now have the organizing ideas for your presentation. Everything else from here on needs to serve you getting this message across to your audience

• •

Make them feel something

Once you know what you want your audience to *know*, the next step is to get clear on how you want them to *feel*. Your emotional intention. You need to make time to consider the emotional journey you are going to take people on. How will they feel after your presentation compared to how they felt at the beginning? In the world of business this is something that's often overlooked. In the worlds of film and theatre it's at the heart of the creative process. It's what transforms an audience's experience, moving it from something purely transactional into something transformational.

If we accept the premise that any presentation is an act of selling, an attempt to get someone to buy or buy-into an idea, then it's essential that we consider this emotional element. Buying decisions are not exclusively logical. Even the most analytical audience are susceptible to emotional influence. In a pitch context organizations employ all sorts of procurement procedures to try to reduce this but until we start pitching to robots, human beings will always have an emotional reaction to the words that they hear, no matter how hard they try to suppress it.

When we find ourselves in front of an audience, whether it's an audience of one or one thousand, there is an unconscious set of processes at play. As they are listening to what we say, they are automatically filtering our message and having an emotional reaction to it. From boredom and despair, through to excitement and elation, our words have an effect whether we like it or not. Rather than leaving things up to chance and hoping for the best, if we can get specific about what we want them to *feel* we are much more likely to take them on an emotional journey.

For an actor in the rehearsal room this idea of emotional intention is commonplace. For every script I worked on from drama school onwards, I spent hours contemplating what my character was trying to make the other characters in the scene feel, then annotating my script accordingly. I'd choose a different emotional intention for almost every line to help me bring the words to life. But it's not a trick. It's something that actors have codified from real life. Since you uttered your first sound as a baby you learned how the noise coming out of your mouth had an impact on those around you. If you cried or screamed someone fed you or changed you, if you gurgled and cooed someone smiled back or tickled your tummy.

As adults we follow the same steps without a second thought. If we want something to happen and we don't seem to be getting our way, or if we find that what we are doing doesn't have the desired effect, we change our tactics. We do something different in order to make those listening feel something new. Anyone who has a teenage child, or can remember being a teenage child, knows how quickly and powerfully the emotional dynamic of a conversation can shift and the impact that has. Most of the time it's completely unconscious but from a communications perspective when we make it deliberate it's incredibly powerful.

The technique that actors use and the one I suggest you employ too is the use of active verbs, doing words, to bring your key messages to life. Are you trying to excite the audience? Or challenge them? Or reassure them? This makes it an active process, something you do to your audience. How you feel as the person speaking is irrelevant. It's all about them. It doesn't matter, for example, how excited you are about the topic you are talking about, what matters is how excited the audience feel about it.

When I worked as an actor, I was also lucky enough to be invited to be a guest teacher at some of the UK's leading drama schools. I'd always tell my students that emotional intention was the difference between good acting and bad acting. A bad actor showed you how they were feeling, a good actor made the other characters in the scene and the audience feel something. It's a subtle distinction but an important one.

You need to think about how your audience are likely to be feeling about you and your topic when you first open your mouth to speak, and how you want them to be feeling when you utter the final words of your presentation. How will it change as you navigate through your key messages?

There's no set way of doing this. The choice is yours. It's what will make the audience experience unique. What is the emotional journey you want to take them on? Will you start by *challenging* them, go on to *educate* them and finish by *uplifting* them? Or will you begin by *reassuring* them, then *intriguing* them and end by *surprising* them?

Think of this shift in emotional intention as a gear change, something that will stop the experience flatlining for the audience. Whilst actors pick something new for almost every line, in a presentation context I'd suggest much broader brush strokes. It might make sense to attach a different emotional intention to each of your key messages. Or, if time is short, it may be more appropriate to focus on one emotional intention for the whole thing. As a rule of thumb, I'd be looking for some sort of shift every five minutes or so. Think of it like a piece of music. Listening to the same song on loop for an hour would probably get pretty monotonous. Like the soundtrack to a blockbuster movie, a great DJ set, or the movements in a classical symphony, there needs to be highs and lows, a shift in mood and energy.

The great thing about this technique is that it has a double impact. It will definitely change the tone of your communication and how you say the words but if you really commit to it, it will actually change the words you use too. If you want to try to *excite* someone, you'll be using completely different language than if you try to *scare* them, even if the topic is the same. That's what makes it such a powerful tool at this stage in the process. Spend time up front deciding what you want them to *feel* and it will help you chose what to say and will even help you filter things like supporting imagery and case studies too.

Regardless of how many gear-changes you plan, what's most important is deciding how you want to leave people feeling at the end of your presentation. This is what your whole performance will build to. The emotional resonance you create will live on long after they have forgotten the detail of what you said, so be strategic in your choices. It's the difference between something that's completely forgettable or memorable for all the right reasons.

Table 2 shows a list of some emotional intentions that might be useful for presentations and pitches. It's by no means exhaustive and I'd encourage you to augment it as you start to implement the technique. Some of them may seem quite similar but what's important is what the words mean to you. Afterall, it's you who needs to bring them to life. It's unlikely that your audience would use exactly the same words as you chose if you were to ask them

Table 2 Emotional intentions

Alarm	Convert	Harness	Restrain
Align	Convince	Ignite	Rouse
Animate	Dare	Implore	Scare
Applaud	Delight	Impress	Sell
Assure	Dissuade	Influence	Shame
Awaken	Dominate	Inspire	Shock
Boost	Educate	Instruct	Stimulate
Brighten	Encourage	Intrigue	Surprise
Cajole	Energise	Involve	Teach
Caution	Enliven	Motivate	Tempt
Celebrate	Entice	Persuade	Threaten
Challenge	Excite	Praise	Touch
Charm	Fascinate	Protect	Unite
Comfort	Focus	Provoke	Uplift
Compliment	Frighten	Reassure	Vitalize
Congratulate	Flatter	Reprimand	Wow

how they felt when you finish speaking but if you've done your job well it will be somewhere in the right ballpark.

Don't just rely on the list in Table 2. There are thousands of active verbs to choose from so start creating a list of your own. To make sure you're using a verb and not an emotional state, simply insert the word into this sentence: 'Can my audience feel (verb)ed?' If the answer is yes, you're on the right track. An audience can't feel 'confident*ed*' for example, but they can feel 'impressed'.

Once you've decided on your emotional intention it's time to turn your attention to your behavioural intention.

STAND & DELIVER

• •

WHAT DO YOU WANT YOUR AUDIENCE TO *FEEL*?

On a piece of paper write down the emotional journey you want to take your audience on during your pitch and presentation. Refer to Table 2 – which words jump out at you?

If your presentation is five minutes or less, choose the one word that describes how you would like to leave your audience feeling.

If your presentation is longer, think about the gear changes you would like to go through? How do you want them to feel when you start? What is the emotion you are looking to elicit at the end? What other notes will you hit as you go through the body of the presentation?

Once you've written them down, use them to help you choose what to include and what to leave out. As you look at the list, does the emotional journey flow for the audience? An emotional journey that moves from one extreme to another is more powerful and engaging than one that feels repetitive and predictable. Remember that when you commit fully, the emotional intention will influence not only the way that you deliver the message but the language and the content that you use as well.

• •

Don't be afraid to ask

Making an ask of your audience doesn't come naturally to most people. We don't want to come across as too pushy or 'salesy'. But if you don't make what you're asking for explicit, how can you expect anyone to say yes? Your behavioural intention is all about the action you want people to take as a result of listening to you speak. It's the answer to the question 'what do I want my audience to *do*?'. Another useful way to think of it is as a 'call to action' (often abbreviated to CTA in the world of marketing).

If you've done the work during the DISCOVER phase to clearly visualize what success looks like, distilling it down to a simple call to action to build your presentation around should be relatively easy. Your job is to articulate your 'ask' in simple terms – and to make sure it's not buried, but front and centre. It's about guiding your thinking as you build the presentation and guiding your audience's thinking as they listen to it.

Every pitch or presentation has one, even if it's not obvious at first. The trick is to keep it simple. The behavioural intention of a 'project update' presentation might be for your boss to trust you to keep going with what you're doing without further intervention. Whilst the 'call to action' might seem more obvious for a more formal pitch or sales presentation, the danger is making things too broad. Rather than the intention being 'to get them to say yes' or 'sign the contract', it's more useful to think about what I call the 'logical next step'. Do you want them to book another meeting or introduce you to the key decision maker for example? Breaking your behavioural intention down into these more bite-sized chunks using the 'logical next step' concept is a much more effective way of working. It stops you thinking in broad brushstrokes and forces you to be specific, which in turn helps the audience to act.

The 'call to action' or 'logical next step' have a natural home at the end of the conversation but to increase the likelihood of your audience doing what you want them to, it's always a good idea to seed things throughout. Either explicitly stating early on what you will be asking for at the end or gently hinting at what you're hoping for all the way through. Personally, I'm a fan of a dual approach where you set things out early on – which gives you a chance to handle any audience surprises or objections upfront – and then reinforce the 'ask' subtly as you work your way through the presentation.

Whichever approach you take in the final presentation, the importance of clearly defining your behavioural intention during the DISTIL phase can't be overstated. It will help you focus your content and messaging in a streamlined way, leaving less room for tangents. The focus it provides will also work to reduce 'off topic' questions from the audience which can easily derail things. Just like with your headline, being economical with your words is really important here too. The cleaner and more concise your 'ask', the easier it is for you to make it!

Once you're clear on what you want them to *do*, you need to give some thought to why the time for action is *now*.

 STAND & DELIVER

WHAT DO YOU WANT YOUR AUDIENCE TO *DO*?

In fewer than 30 words write down what you want your audience to *do* at the end of the pitch or presentation. What is the 'logical next step' you want them to take? Now reduce it to fewer than 15 words using the following sentence structure: 'I want my audience to…':

- I want my audience to give me a pay rise
- I want my audience to agree to a meeting next week
- I want my audience to sign off on the budget for the project
- I want my audience to appoint our firm as their advisor

Now think about where you will position this ask in your presentation. Will you wait until the end? Or will you also make the 'ask' early to help frame the conversation and make your request clear? Keep referring back to your 'call to action' as you build your narrative.

Make it 'towards' or 'away from'

Being able to articulate what we want our audience to do is one thing. Getting them to actually do it is a whole different ball game! We need to get inside their heads and understand what makes them tick. We have to be able to articulate why now is the time to change, to consider our message, to take action, or to explore a new perspective. If we can't create that sense of urgency for our audience, they are very unlikely to do anything.

Think of your own to-do list right now. I guarantee that there are things on there that are important but not urgent and consistently get bumped when other more urgent things come along. Urgent and important is the sweet spot for rapid action. To tap into this, we need to understand how our audience is motivated when it comes to the topic or idea we are presenting. Luckily when it comes to motivation there are only two options. People are motivated 'towards' or 'away from'.

People with 'towards' motivation are focused on the goal or the outcome. They know what they're looking to achieve and want your help getting them there. You'll hear them using words like 'win', 'obtain', 'achieve' and they'll talk about their objectives, timelines and goals.

People with 'away from' motivation are focused on the pain they want to avoid. They're looking to protect themselves from harm but will only act if the danger of inaction is greater than the potential risk of doing something about it. You'll hear them using words like 'problems', 'obstacles', 'issues' and they'll talk about the difficulties they want to solve and the situations they want to avoid.

To motivate a 'towards' audience you need to help them see the urgency of taking steps today, why action is necessary now in order for them to achieve their desired outcome. For an 'away from' motivated audience you'll need to dial up the pain of staying still and focus on all the bad stuff that will be avoided by doing the thing you are asking them to do.

It's quite possible, especially in a pitch context or when speaking to a large audience that you won't know for certain whether your audience is motivated 'towards' or 'away from'. In this scenario, your job is to paint a picture of both the benefit of taking action and the pain of staying still. If you can articulate why the time for action is now, you're halfway to getting your audience to take the first step.

Now you know what you want your audience to *know*, *feel* and *do*, and you can articulate why *now* is the time to do it. Next, you need to consider how to bring your message to life.

 STAND & DELIVER

● ●

WHY *NOW*?

Take a blank piece of paper and divide it in two. It's time to work out what could be motivating your audience so you can help them answer the questions 'why *now*?'. At the top of the left-hand column write the word 'Towards'. At the top of the right-hand column write the words 'Away From'.

Now get to work.

In the 'Toward' column list all the positive reasons people would want to take action. The benefits of moving quickly.

In the 'Away From' column list all the pain that your audience will want to avoid. Build a compelling case for steering clear of the negatives.

Look at the list you have created and decide which are the most compelling things to focus on in your presentation. The more you can amplify the pain and the rewards the more likely your words are to land.

● ●

Add some stardust

Now that your presentation has the building blocks of an intellectual, emotional and behavioural intention it's time to decide how you will bring it to life. You don't have to decide on how everything fits together at this stage, but you want to gather the key elements that you are going to use. Like a film director creating a movie you decide on all the shots and components you think you'll need in advance – the close ups, the wides, the mid-shots, the music, the special effects, etc – but you don't put them together until you get into the editing suite.

Another way of thinking about it is like a chef creating a new dish. You have an idea of the flavour combinations you want produce, the raw ingredients you will include, a rough way they will fit together but you need to go through lots of experimentation and tweaking before you have a recipe that gives you a replicable result. In this DISTIL phase we are still experimenting with the flavours and gathering our ingredients. We'll worry about the exact recipe, the seasoning and the visual presentation later on.

What we're looking for at this stage is 'stardust' – those things that will make your audience sit up and listen. These are the things that will be memorable long after you have left the room. The things that add credibility and gravitas to your message. Of all the things you brainstormed in the DISCOVER phase, what feels like it makes the cut now that you have a clear sense of what you want your audience to *know*, *feel* and *do*? There are a few categories I suggest you consider.

Facts and figures

Let's start with the data. What are some of the big numbers that stand out? Are there any important facts that need to be included? This category of 'stardust' will especially appeal to any 'head' energy people in the audience. At this stage avoid getting too much into the detail. Think about the data that supports your headline and subheadings. What is the key evidence that reinforces your message? How do you make it as relatable for your audience as possible? Just because you understand it inside-out and back-to-front doesn't mean that they will!

Case-studies and stories

What are some of the more human ways of reinforcing your argument. Have you got examples of how what you're suggesting has worked in other scenarios? Case-studies and real-life examples are incredibly powerful ways to illustrate what you are talking about. Are there stories you could include to bring things to life? These could be personal anecdotes of how you have done something, reinforcing your own credibility. Or they could be stories about your organization, product or service. We'll look at how to structure these properly later. At this stage it's just about choosing which ones work best to reinforce your key messages.

Visuals

Different audience members will have different preferences for consuming information, so I always recommend you include compelling visuals in any pitch or presentation. What images help reinforce what you are saying? Avoid 'clip art' and obvious, generic stock imagery if you can. The more specific and tailored the visuals, the more impactful they will be. That doesn't mean they have to be obvious though; abstract imagery can work well to reinforce the concepts you are talking about. Video is another powerful tool but try to keep it punchy. Long, repetitive or generic video can give your audience a chance to zone out rather than keeping them focused on your messaging. The same is true of product demos too. Don't lose people in the detail, keep things moving and engaging to avoid leaving people feeling overwhelmed.

Testimonials and social proof

Dr Robert Cialdini talks about the concept of 'social proof' in his seminal book *Influence*.[4] The idea is very simple: 'one means we use to determine what is correct is to find out what other people think is correct'. We're more likely to engage with something if other people have endorsed it first. The book itself has sold over five million copies which, in itself, provides social proof for the concept of social proof! What others have to say about us is much more impactful than anything we could say about ourselves or our ideas. Do you have any testimonials that support your pitch? What do clients and customers say about working with you or the results that you have generated for them? Are there other people you can leverage to reinforce your ideas? Who can you quote or reference to give more gravitas to your message?

Metaphor and simile

If you take yourself back to studying English at school, you'll remember your teacher talking about the power of metaphor and simile. Great writers use this powerful literary device to transport their audience on a journey of imagination. In a pitch or presentation context it can be useful to do the same. Is there a unifying idea you can build your narrative around? Is what you're talking about 'like' something else that your audience already understand?

Film producer Charlie Fink is famously credited as pitching *The Lion King* to Disney using three words: 'Bambi in Africa'.[5] It's brilliantly simple and instantly allows the audience to understand the concept. How can you articulate some of the complex elements of your pitch and presentation by using a simple metaphor?

Once you've decided on the 'stardust' you want to include – any facts, figures, case-studies, stories, visuals, testimonials, social proofs, metaphors or similes that support your key messages – it's time to decide on the structure you will use to hold it all together.

Use the blockbuster formula

A great pitch or presentation is like a well-crafted piece of entertainment. Your audience should be able to sit back, relax and enjoy the show. You want them fully engaged but not having to work too hard. The experience should be frictionless, and they should get to the end ready to take action and wanting more. It's a delicate balance.

Broadly speaking, in the world of film you have two types of movies: blockbuster and art-house. Blockbusters follow a logical narrative, there's plenty of action and suspense but it's not too difficult to join the dots. They follow a simple timeline, the characters are well defined, you have a clear sense of where things are going but it's not so obvious you zone out. These films appeal to a wide audience and normally take lots of money at the box office but don't often win awards.

Art-house, or indie movies as they are sometimes known, are normally more complex. They might not follow a conventional timeline. There might be multiple plots. They tend to make the audience work harder to understand what's going on and can leave you with more questions than answers. These films often win awards but tend to appeal to a more niche audience and take less money at the box office.

When we apply these distinctions in the world of pitching and presenting, 99% of the time we want to be more blockbuster. We want to make it easy for our audience. We need to do the hard work so that they don't have to. Art-house style presentations might seem clever and interesting, but you run a real risk of your audience zoning out and switching off, which is an instant recipe for failure.

So, what's the secret to a presentation structure that cuts through? The good news is that when you look at blockbuster movies you begin to notice a pattern. A way of structuring the narrative that we can use to keep our audience engaged and wanting more.

Consciously or unconsciously, many of us have come across the concept of the three-act structure popularized by Joseph Campbell in his book, *A Hero with a Thousand Faces*.[6] The hero's journey has a clear beginning, middle and end. Or as they are known in screen writing circles – a *setup*, a *confrontation* and a *resolution*. This simple way of organizing the action allows us to effortlessly engage with the experience of the hero of the story. It's a formula that's hidden in plain sight. People will happily part with their money in order to engage with it over and over again.

Have you ever watched a movie from one of the great blockbuster movie franchises? A Bond film? A Harry Potter instalment? A Star Wars movie? One of the Marvel series? Most of us have. If you've seen more than one, you're living proof of the power of this formula. If we're honest with ourselves, at a macro level the movies in these franchises are all exactly the same. We already know roughly what is going to happen and yet, time and again we buy our ticket and our popcorn, sit back and enjoy the show, eagerly anticipating what is coming next. Why wouldn't we want the audiences in our presentations doing the same?

In the *setup* of a movie things generally start with a bang to grab our attention and we then go on to discover all the important details: where the action is set, who the main characters are, what problems they are facing, what they're looking to achieve, who's good, who's bad, the reason that change is needed, etc.

If we use the Bond franchise as an example we begin with a car chase, a gun fight or some other high-octane event before going on to discover where in the world the story is set, who the baddie is, what mission 007 is on and who the potential love interest is.

The *confrontation* is then a series of trials and tribulations that move the hero incrementally towards their goal. The path is rarely linear and there will be setbacks along the way but little by little they take steps in the right direction.

If we go back to the world of 007 the *confrontation* section of a Bond movie sees our hero come dangerously close to being wiped out by the villain. There will be several chases, fights and skirmishes thrown in for good measure and James will inevitably become ensnared in a love story that threatens to derail his success.

The *resolution* is where all the loose ends get tied up and good normally triumphs over evil. We're left celebrating success with a vision for a brave new world. This all happens quite quickly once the final hurdle has been surmounted, giving us a feeling that everyone will live happily ever after.

Back in the world of James Bond this is where the villain is defeated and for a moment we have a feeling of hope that everything will work out ok. Normality is restored and we see our hero sipping a cocktail gazing out across the sunset.

But what has any of this got to do with the structure of a pitch or presentation? Quite a lot as it happens!

The *setup* is where we set the context. What is the question or problem that our presentation is solving? What does our audience need to know about us? What are some of the big ideas we are going to grapple with? What can our audience expect from us as the presentation unfolds?

The *confrontation* makes up the bulk of our presentation or pitch. We need to avoid the negative connotation of the word here and see this section instead as an opportunity to share our best thinking. It's where we lay out our argument, evaluate the pros and cons, put forward different options for consideration, as well as the data, stories and case studies that support our narrative.

Finally, the *resolution* is our conclusion. The 'call to action' where we deliver our verdict and suggest the next steps. In a formal pitch it's where we ask for the business. In a presentation it's where we encourage our audience to act based on what they've just heard.

When we look at the most successful films a ratio begins to emerge for how these three sections fit together. A rule of thumb for how long to spend on each part. The *setup* is roughly 20% of the whole, the *confrontation* 70% and the *resolution* 10%. We take time up front to set the scene, give most of our focus to the main action and then get things over and done with quickly. You've never seen James Bond take his suit to the dry cleaners or his Aston Martin to the car wash!

This 20:70:10 ratio is the ideal superstructure for any presentation or pitch. You don't have to stick to it doggedly but if you've got ten minutes you should spend roughly two minutes on the *setup* providing context, seven minutes on the *confrontation* working through your various arguments and ideas, and one minute on the *resolution* wrapping everything up with a clear call to action. If you've got 30 minutes it's six minutes in the *setup*, 21 minutes in the *confrontation* and three minutes in the *resolution* and so on.

The great thing about this magic ratio is that it's invisible to your audience. You may notice it now that you know it's there, but if you've sat through any of the movies I've mentioned above, I'd be very surprised if you were consciously aware of the three acts. Instead, the structure unconsciously aided your enjoyment. As the film moves from one section to the next, the familiar pattern helps you savour the story and anticipate what's coming next.

It's worth noting that if you've been given specific questions to answer, in a specific order (which is common in procurement led pitches), you should do as you are asked. Instead ensure you weave in some sort of *setup* and *resolution* into the opening and closing sections to set the context and deliver a strong conclusion.

However, assuming you're given 'carte blanche' in terms of structure, the allocation of time using the 20:70:10 ratio will transform your presentations in an instant. Now you've got a superstructure to work with, it's time to craft your content for maximum cut-through.

 STAND & DELIVER

• •

20:70:10

Use the 20:70:10 structure to work out the rough timings for your pitch or presentation. Allocate 20% of your total time to the *setup*, 70% to the *confrontation* and 10% to the *resolution*.

If you're expected to have dedicated time for Q&A take this off the total time before applying the ratio to the remainder. Do this even if you intend to incorporate the Q&A time throughout (which we will discuss later) as you really don't want questions during your *setup* or *resolution.*

Example:	60 minutes total presentation time including 10 minutes Q&A = 50 minutes of planned content
	Setup = 10 minutes *Confrontation* = 35 minutes *Resolution* = 5 minutes

The expectation here isn't that you'll stick to these timings exactly but that they will guide your planning of the presentation.

Write the section timings down and roughly allocate the elements you have planned so far against them. Do you have enough time for everything that you are currently planning to include? Very often the answer is no. If that's the case, you need to decide what can be left out.

• •

Chapter summary

The second step of this playbook has been focused on refining your messaging and your content. Sometimes it can be a challenge to strip things back in this way, as our instinct tells us that the more we include, the more knowledgeable and impressive we appear. However, we need to remember that simplicity is one of the key ingredients of cut-through. We must also remember that none of this is about us. Great pitches and presentations are focused on the audience. It's all about giving them exactly what they need. The more streamlined and coherent your narrative, the easier it will be for your audience to follow your logic and for you to lead them towards the outcome you are looking for.

To complete this phase of the process you need to do the following:

- ✓ Choose your format. Is this a feature film or a box set?
- ✓ Decide on your headline and three to five key messages
- ✓ Decide on the emotional journey you want to take the audience on
- ✓ Decide on your 'call to action' or the 'logical next step' you will ask for
- ✓ Articulate why now is the time for action
- ✓ Choose the 'stardust' that will help bring your message to life
- ✓ Apply the blockbuster formula to your content to see what stays and what goes

Getting clear and refined in your messaging before you start committing to scripts and slide design will mean that everything comes together with greater ease and impact. You'll avoid constantly reworking and reordering. Once you've done all the hard thinking, it's time to get creative and decide how to bring your narrative to life.

Chapter three

DESIGN: Craft a blockbuster narrative

Step 3: Design

You've diligently refined what you want to say and gathered all the essentials for a great pitch or presentation. You're clear on your intentions and know exactly what your key messages are. The time has come to focus on the DESIGN phase. This is not just about designing the visuals (if you choose to use them) but designing the exact narrative you will follow. It's time to get creative and to pull everything together into a presentation that will wow your audience.

As I've mentioned already this is the step that many people, mistakenly, try to start with but if you've followed the process so far, you now have all the ingredients of something special. This is where we start to bring things to life. Think of it like the edit of a great movie. This is where you can start moving things around for maximum impact, adding some metaphorical special FX and music, and generally sharpening the narrative to maximize your influence.

With a 20:70:10 superstructure in place the DESIGN phase is where we add the detail and decide precisely what goes into each of the three acts. By the end of it you will know exactly what you are saying and have all the supporting materials so that you can start to rehearse and develop your performance.

Always go back to the exam question

I know you're champing at the bit to get going and bring the presentation together but before you do, a word of warning: *make sure you're answering the exam question*.

Right at the beginning of this book I recommended that you shouldn't be afraid to say no. That you should only take on the demands of a pitch or presentation if you felt you could give a compelling answer to the question being posed. If you've got to this stage in the process, my assumption is that you feel you do. The trick is to keep that question front of mind as you build everything else.

Every word that you write, every image that you show, every prop that you use should be in service of answering that question. If it doesn't help you answer the question, leave it out. There are no prizes for going off on tangents. Keep everything sharp and focused. If it helps, write the exam question in bold letters somewhere prominent and keep it in your field of vision as you work through the next steps.

Now that we've cleared that up let's talk about scripts.

Decide on how to script it

To script? Or not to script? That, is the question.

As an actor, one of the hardest parts of the job was learning the lines. What was even harder was then speaking them aloud in such a way that the audience believed they were coming out of your mouth for the first time. It's a real skill. And a skill that most people don't possess. Why should they?! If we're in the audience of a pitch or presentation we don't want to see the person in front of us putting on an act, we want to see them authentically and confidently communicating with us.

Actors get paid to learn lines and it takes time. But we don't always have time when we're prepping a presentation. I've worked with a lot of people that didn't want to let go of their script. They'd crafted their narrative word for word and wanted to read it so that nothing got left out. The switch to online meetings during the Covid pandemic played a big part in this too. People got comfortable having their notes on the screen in front of them as a safety net. Unfortunately, despite leaving the person presenting feeling more secure, it is a tactic that unwittingly leads to a less engaging experience for the audience.

I completely understand the desire to fully script what you want to say. In fact, it's something that I like to do myself if I have time. But I don't recommend you stop when you've got all the words down. Instead, I'd encourage you to strip it back as you rehearse and refine things down to key sentences, phrases and eventually just key words. This will give you much more flexibility and make the final delivery much more real and engaging.

Fully scripted presentations really don't serve you. It's incredibly difficult to bring the text to life. If you haven't learnt it, it's really challenging to engage with your audience as you read. If you have learnt it, when you inevitably slip up, miss a couple of words or someone asks you an unexpected question, there's a high chance that everything comes crashing down and you lose where you are, breaking the flow and your rapport with the audience.

My favoured approach is to use frameworks. Think of them like scaffolding for your presentation. A structure to build from that gives you the reassurance of knowing where you are but that is invisible to your audience. You can fill in all the details and fully script things using frameworks if you need to, but as you become more and more familiar with your content the frameworks will allow you to know what's coming next without the need to write down every single word. If you don't have time for hours and hours of preparation you can also use a framework to decide on the big picture narrative, ensuring that you can navigate elegantly and engagingly through your content.

After many years experimenting with different frameworks I now have a go-to beginning and end – the 20% and the 10%. For the 70% in the middle, I use a range of different three-part structures depending on the purpose of the presentation. I'll explain what each of the elements is as I take you through the DESIGN phase in the sections that follow. I may tweak and adjust elements as I develop my narrative, but this is always my jumping-off point and helps me have a consistent approach to putting a presentation together.

I also recommend starting with big picture structuring first rather than reaching for the PowerPoint or writing out the script. By all means, if you plan to use slides, dump ideas into a document as you go, but don't spend any time finessing the visuals until you have the narrative right. Sticky notes work brilliantly as you experiment with the structure because they make it really easy to move things round and you can use different colours for different things to help you get a visual representation for the flow of what you're going to say.

Figure 5 is a useful guide for how to structure your content and bring your thinking together.

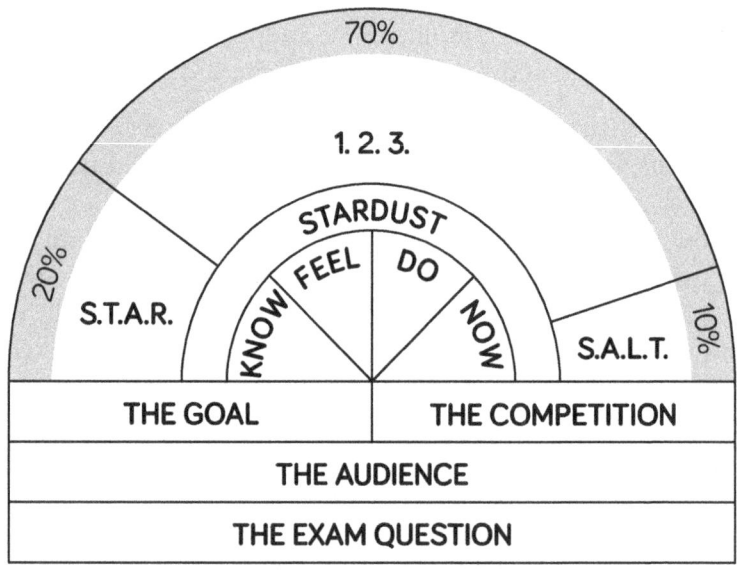

Figure 5 The Cut-Through formula

You identified The Exam Question and got clear on The Audience, The Goal and The Competition in the DECIDE phase. You refined your answers to *Know?*, *Feel?*, *Do?* and *Now?*, then gathered your Stardust in the DISTIL phase. In this DESIGN phase we're going to bring it all together with a *S.T.A.R.* opening, *S.A.L.T.* to close and a *1.2.3.* middle section. Let's get started.

Brilliant beginnings

First impressions are everything. Cut-through starts with the very first words you utter. If you don't grab your audience's attention immediately you've lost them. There are too many distractions. There are too many options. There are too many things competing for their attention. They have to know you have begun.

Be honest with yourself. How often have you sat in a meeting room or a conference hall looking at something on your phone or chatting to the person next to you only to discover that presentation has begun without you even noticing? You failed to spot that the speaker had started. What I'm about to say may sound harsh but in that instance you, the audience member, were not at fault. The responsibility for your inattention lies solely with the speaker.

So often, people warm up into a presentation. They spend the first few minutes finding their feet. They cover the unimportant stuff before they get to the important stuff. This approach won't serve you. Instead, you have to signpost clearly that you've begun. Demanding your audience's attention immediately is scary. It thrusts you straight into the spotlight. But it's the only way to guarantee people sit up and listen.

Research from the University of York suggests it takes as little as 33 milliseconds for an audience to judge our trustworthiness, status and attractiveness.[1] Our impact is almost instantaneous, so the first words that come out of our mouths really count. If you kick things off with inconsequential small talk or, as I often see, caveats and apologies, your audience will quickly switch off. You need to be more interesting than whatever they are currently engaging with or thinking about. They have to know you've started. The best way I've found to ensure that this happens is to use a *S.T.A.R.* opening.

- ▶ **S**urprise
- ▶ **T**akeaways
- ▶ **A**uthority
- ▶ **R**oadmap

Start with a surprise

As I've mentioned already, your first task when opening a pitch or presentation is to let your audience know that you've begun. Don't be tempted to start with small talk or agendas. It needs to be something that will make people sit up and pay attention. There will be time for the agenda later and there's absolutely nothing wrong with some rapport building chit chat as you enter the room. But when you decide the time has come to begin, your audience needs to know you mean business.

For clarity a 'surprise' doesn't have to be something spectacular. There's no need to pull a rabbit out of a hat (unless you're giving a presentation on magic!) or to do anything outrageous. Instead, your job is to work *against* your audience's expectations. Most presentations people experience commence with a slightly rambling segway into the core content. People often make an apologetic start, introduce themselves and the topic, talk about the fire exits or pull up an agenda slide and read it to the audience. All of this is forgettable at best. At worst it gives people listening the perfect excuse to ignore you. They know nothing that you're saying is important, so they can carry on with what they were doing guilt-free.

The good news is you don't have to try too hard to be different from 99% of the other people out there pitching their ideas. The trick is finding a 'surprise' that works in the context of the presentation you are giving and the audience you are talking to. There are numerous ways you could approach this. Here are a few ideas.

A story

Starting with a story or a case-study can be a great way to make your audience take an immediate imaginative leap into the subject matter you are there to discuss. Stories work brilliantly for conveying your message but if you use one at the beginning of a presentation make sure it's pithy and that it's clear how it relates to the topic you are there to discuss. You don't want your audience thinking they're in the wrong room! Ideally aim for something around 60 seconds in length to help you set the scene.

A question

Posing a rhetorical question can be a great way to focus the minds of your audience. What do you want them to consider or reflect on before you take them on the journey of your presentation? You can of course elicit immediate responses from the audience, but this is a more high-risk strategy as their answers present the possibility of pulling you off track. Again, make the question relevant to the topic, not just 'how is everyone this morning?' but something like 'given the challenges we're facing as a business right now what's the best way to secure our long-term future?'.

A quote

Sharing someone else's words at the beginning of a presentation not only encourages your audience to engage with the topic at hand but it also allows you to borrow credibility from the person you are quoting. Once again brevity is your friend here. Reciting paragraphs of someone else's words can easily switch your audience off. However, choosing a deeply relevant sentence or two from a public figure or an expert in the field you will be speaking about, is a great way to frame what comes next.

A figure

Especially for more analytical audiences, using data can be a very powerful way to grab people's attention. Find a headline number or statistic from your presentation and place it upfront. It could be something that encapsulates the problem you are looking to solve e.g. '30% of the customers we surveyed were unhappy with our service'. Or it could be related to the solution you are proposing e.g. 'A $25 investment per month saves the average customer 12 hours a week.' Avoid complicated graphs and spreadsheets at this point. You job is to whet your audience's appetite; the detail can come later on.

A fact

An interesting fact can be a compelling way to start, sparking curiosity and engagement from the audience. Choose something linked to your key messages to focus people's attention on the topic you're going to expand upon. Quite often this approach can be combined with a question for even more impact. 'Did you know…?' with the rest of the presentation going on to expand on why the fact you chose is so important, what it means to the audience and what action they should take as a result of discovering this new information.

An image or a video

An alternative but equally surprising way to start is to use an image or a video. Is there a visual metaphor that would get the audience thinking? Do you have a short video that would set the scene for what you're about to cover? The great thing about this approach is that, done well, whatever you use can do some of the heavy lifting for you. If you get this right, especially when using video, you can trigger an emotional response in your audience which sets the tone for what's to come.

The list above is not exhaustive and there are many ways to start with a 'surprise'. Whichever you choose, your aim should be a signal to your audience that they should be paying attention and to lay the groundwork for what is to come in the rest of the presentation.

Tell them the takeaways

Now that your audience are listening you have to make sure that they don't stop. The best way to maintain their engagement is to step into their shoes. Think back to the last time you sat in the audience during a pitch or a presentation. What was the question going through your head as the presenter started speaking? If you're honest, the question at the back of your mind was a variation on 'what's in it for me?'. You may not have even been consciously aware of it but as you sat and listened your brain was trying to work out whether what you were listening to was useful or relevant.

Your audience isn't being rude. They're just busy. If you can make a compelling case for why they should give you their attention early on they're much less likely to get distracted as things progress. This is the perfect time to give them a sense of exactly what they'll get from spending time with you. 'Over the course of the next 25 minutes, we show you exactly how you can optimize your recruitment process and cut your costs in half' or 'During this update I'm going to demonstrate why using the new team portal will save you time when submitting your expenses.'

The great thing about positioning the 'takeaways' early is it demonstrates to your audience the value they will get from listening to you and creates curiosity. On the flip side it also allows them to quickly evaluate whether what you're going to say is a complete waste of their time. Although your aim isn't to get your audience to push back or walk out, it's much better to discover any problems upfront. You don't want both parties sitting there, hoping that the content will eventually be relevant, only to discover right at the end that it absolutely wasn't. Clarifying the 'takeaways' upfront is good for you and your audience.

Articulate your authority

This part of your introduction is all about credibility. Why are you the right person to be talking about this topic? How can you give your audience comfort that you're worth listening to? Rather than taking time to talk about yourself right at the start, I suggest waiting until this point in the opening to formally introduce yourself. Up until now your audience have been too preoccupied with the 'what's in it for me?' question to care about who you are or what you've achieved. If you've done your job well, following the steps above, they should now be much more open to finding out about you.

If you're pitching as part of a team, this is the moment to go round and get everyone to say a sentence or two about themselves. Keep it short and relevant. If you're presenting solo, you need to decide how much you are going to share about yourself. It will all be context specific of course but don't make the mistake of selling yourself short. The audience want to know that they're in a safe pair of hands. The more you can share your experience and qualifications in a humble and honest way, the more confidence they will have in the words that follow.

As I mentioned, when we talked about celebrating your uniqueness in the DISCOVER phase, many people I work with are uncomfortable about doing this. They don't want to be seen as boastful or arrogant. In reality, being able to share what makes you unique and why people should listen to you is an act of generosity towards your audience. You're putting their minds at ease and reassuring them that you have a level of expertise in what you're about to share.

Sometimes at this point a feeling of imposter syndrome kicks in, especially if you are younger or more junior than your audience. Try to remember that if you have been asked to speak it is because you have knowledge that others can learn from. You may not have been in the industry as long as some of the people listening but, when it come to the topic you're about to talk about, you've got valuable information to share. In a sales context you'll know your product or service in a way that your customers and prospects can't. In a team context you'll have more insight into your area of responsibility than anyone else. Even in a knowledge sharing context, if you're one page ahead of everyone else in the textbook, you still have the upper hand.

There may of course be instances where you already know your audience and it would feel very odd to give a formal introduction but that doesn't mean you should skip this part of the opening. This step is all about demonstrating credibility. Is there something about your experience that your audience are unaware of, which positions you well to talk about this topic. For example, 'Most of you will be unaware that I actually studied mathematics at university, so I'm delighted to take you through the numbers today'. And if you don't have an obvious qualification or historic experience specific to the topic, you can also borrow credibility from others, for example 'I'd like to thank Ali for asking me to lead on this topic this afternoon'.

Whatever words you choose, the more you can draw connections between your experience and your audience, the more they will trust what you say next. Keep it simple and relatable. That's also why I'd suggest you steer clear of job titles. Most of the time they don't mean anything to people outside of your own organization. Instead tell people about how what you do is relevant to them, their interests, problems or needs.

Reveal the roadmap

You've got their attention, they know what's in it for them, they understand why you're perfectly placed to be talking to them. Now, and only now, is it time to talk them through how you plan to structure the presentation. The 'roadmap' is different from the 'takeaways'. The 'roadmap' is much more practical and procedural. It's where you get to talk them through the agenda, let them know what you're going to be covering and agree on any rules for the interaction.

There are several ways to do this of course. In a sales context, especially if procurement are involved, you'd be wise to lay out exactly what you're planning to talk about and how long it's going to take. You need agreement upfront that your approach will work for your audience, and that they have budgeted the same amount of time as you have. You don't want to get halfway through only to have the key decision maker call time, before you've really landed your message, because they've got another meeting to head to. Sharing timings can really help to put people at ease and help them to focus. Rather than sitting there wondering how long each section will last, they know where they are in the proceedings making it easier to listen.

If you can afford to keep some of your cards closer to your chest, you may opt for a more big-picture approach. Rather than getting into the detail and specifics you can hint at the broad brushstrokes of what people can expect, for example 'Over the course of the next 15 minutes I'd like to talk you through each of the three strategies that have had the biggest impact on this project's success'. This works well when you want to keep your audience on their toes and maintain an element of surprise.

This is also a good point to define what I think of as 'the rules of the game'. I'll talk about this in more detail in the DELIVER phase but essentially you need to frame your expectations about how the pitch or presentation will play out. It's too easy to assume that your audience knows what to do but if you don't make things explicit there's a danger that you end up on different pages. Do you want the session to be interactive? Would you prefer people kept questions until a certain point? If the meeting is virtual, should they raise a digital hand or just unmute their microphone and go for it? It may seem a bit premature but making these decisions now will influence how you plan the rest of your content.

This section of your opening provides a jumping-off point for the main body of your presentation. At the end of it your audience should be crystal clear on what they should expect to hear and how long it's going to take. It also provides an opportunity for clarification and adjustments before you get into your flow. It's much easier to adapt your approach at this early stage than to discover with ten minutes to spare that you've been on completely the wrong track. With the formalities taken care of they'll be much more likely to relax and listen to what you have to say next.

Start with a surprise, tell them the takeaways, articulate your authority, reveal the roadmap (*S.T.A.R.*).

This simple framework allows you to craft a compelling opening that will ensure your audience leans in. When you get to the DRILL stage, it's also a brilliant way to help you master the opening so that you can deliver with impact. Personally, I always find I'm most nervous in the first few minutes of any pitch or presentation. If I don't have a clear strategy, there's a real danger I'll forget what I've planned to say, go off around the houses or speed up and trip over my words. The *S.T.A.R.* opening helps me avoid all those pitfalls. I can use it to craft 12 minutes of opening content and scene setting if I'm giving an hour-long speech. Or I can choose a couple of sentences for each element if I need a two-minute opening for a ten-minute update.

Other openings are available of course but this formula creates cut-through every single time. It's flexible, dynamic and almost invisible to the audience, taking them on a journey that ticks all the right boxes: capturing their attention, showing them why they should listen, giving them confidence in who they're listening to and providing an overview of what they're going to be hearing during the presentation.

Now that you know how to begin, we need to focus on the all-important second act.

 STAND & DELIVER

· ·

CREATE A *S.T.A.R.* OPENING

Take a moment to sketch out a *S.T.A.R.* opening. You don't need to script it in full, although you may want to refine it when the time comes to rehearse. Jot down some bullet-point answers to the questions below.

Surprise

How could you kick things off with a bang? A story? A question? A quote? A fact? A figure? An image? A video? What would work best given the context of your presentation and the audience you will be speaking to?

Takeaways

What are the key takeaways for the audience? What will they get from spending time listening to you? Use the work you have already done during the DISTIL phase on your key messages to help you with this. You don't have to tell them everything but what would really whet their appetite and get your audience leaning in?

Authority

How will you introduce yourself, your organization or your team? What could you say that would demonstrate your expertise and give your audience confidence in your message? If you know your audience well, what new information could you share at this point that would further increase your credibility?

Roadmap

How do you plan to structure your pitch or presentation? What is the agenda you are proposing? How much time have you allocated to each section? What are the 'rules of the game' you are suggesting in terms of engagement and interaction?

The final thing to consider is how long your *S.T.A.R.* opening will to be. Remember it should account for approximately 20% of your presentation. Grab a timer and roughly talk the four sections aloud. How long did it last? What do you need to cut or expand on? Refine your ideas until you have a powerful opening section.

To download a worksheet of these questions to help you craft your *S.T.A.R.* opening visit www.cut-throughbook.com.

Mesmerizing middles

The middle section makes up the main bulk of your pitch or presentation. It's the 70% in the 20:70:10 ratio and it's where you make the case for the key messages you have selected. If we go back to the movie analogy, this is Act 2. It's the *confrontation* where the core of the action unfolds. During this middle section the audience gets the full picture and it's important that you craft a narrative that's compelling and easy to follow.

The objectives, contexts and audiences for pitches and presentations are so varied it would be wrong to suggest a one-size-fits-all approach here. However, the effectiveness of your presentation will largely come down to your ability to structure your thoughts for this all-important middle part in a way that resonates with your audience. You must choose wisely.

In some instances, the audience will dictate exactly how they want the information presented. In many formal procurement-based pitch contexts, for example, the prospect will give you a series of questions they want you to answer. Do as they ask. There are no prizes for not addressing the topics that your audience want you to discuss.

In other contexts, you may be given a broader steer by the person asking you to speak 'please can you give us an update on the progress of the project including any threats and any opportunities' or in a job interview context 'talk to the panel about three experiences that have shaped your career'. In both examples there is an underlying structure, implied by the instruction, that the audience is seeking (progress, threats and opportunities in example 1 and three experiences in example 2).

Again, don't overlook these requests. It's important that you give your audience what they ask for.

There will of course be many instances where the choice of how to structure things is down to you and that's where life get exciting. Don't get carried away though. A constant theme throughout this book has been simplicity and the middle section is no different. Don't pack it with 27 examples to illustrate your point. Or 15 case studies from happy clients. Or 11 ways to implement the strategy. In that direction lies audience overwhelm. Something we want to avoid at all costs. Instead, we want a flexible way of arranging our thinking.

I'd suggest it's a simple as *1.2.3.*

When crafting this middle section of your presentation, if you can use a three-part structure, it will keep you focused and make the argument you are presenting, or the story you are telling, much easier for the audience to understand. As I've already mentioned there are many other ways you could to it but knowing your *1.2.3.* is extremely simple and highly effective. These three elements don't have to be equally weighted. They don't necessarily have to be delivered in order. But if you can collect your ideas into three clear buckets it will help you organize and build your argument.

There are a couple of core *1.2.3.* structures that I would suggest are applicable in a wide variety of situations which I'll take you through in detail shortly.

▷ The first is **Problems – Options – Proposal (POP)**. This is great if you need to create a persuasive argument.

▷ The second is **Past – Present – Future (PPF)**. This is perfect if you want to deliver a more story-based narrative.

There are of course many instances where something more tailored is required so I've also given you ten additional *1.2.3.* structures in *Appendix A: More formulas for a 1.2.3. middle*. These are specifically designed for the most common scenarios that I help clients prepare for: sales pitches, product demos, team updates, project reviews, business cases, town hall/all-hands meetings, project kick offs, strategy presentations, performance reviews and educational presentations.

Before we look at POP and PPF in more detail, let's dig a little deeper into how and why the concept of *1.2.3.* works. First, a three-part structure has a logical flow. For maximum cut-through we must present our material in a way that is easy for our audience to follow. If we confuse them, we lose them. We want to deliver things in a coherent way without disconcerting flashbacks or jumps in the narrative.

It also provides a lot of flexibility. As long as you cover each of the three steps, you can choose what goes into each and how long you spend on them. This allocation should be dictated by the audience and your goal rather than a dogged adherence to a formula. It allows every presentation you create to be different whilst giving you a framework to fall back on.

Finally, this three-step approach to the middle section provides what is known as a liberating constraint. Sometimes too much freedom can be overwhelming. Conversely if we limit our options, we often find it sets us free. Knowing you can't include it all, that you must work within the scaffolding and that you only have a certain amount of time all serve to sharpen your performance. If you watch skilled actors improvising it can seem risky and impulsive but sitting in the background are a series of agreements and frameworks, underlying rules that give invisible order to the chaos. That's what a *1.2.3.* can do for your presentation.

Let's look now at the two core structures you can use in multiple contexts.

Problems – Options – Proposal (POP)

A powerful way to structure the middle of a persuasive presentation (be that a sales pitch, a company update or even a TED talk) is to use the acronym POP: Problems – Options – Proposal. This formula does exactly what it says on the tin and takes the audience from the issue that's been identified, through a series of possible solutions all the way through to the recommendation you are making. Let's break it down a bit further.

Problems

We mustn't shy away from pain. Especially in a sales context but even in a more conventional presentation, if we can get our audience to identify with what is wrong it becomes a catalyst for change. By highlighting the issues that require attention or problems that exist, you help the audience to focus. What is wrong with the current approach? Why is the status quo broken? What are the mistakes that people like your audience often make? In the DISTIL phase we talked about 'towards' and 'away from' motivation. This step is about keying into the audience's desire to move away from what's not working. When we can bring the problem into focus and get our audience to associate with the cost of inaction, they are much more likely to listen to the choices we present them with.

Options

Once you've identified the problem, the obvious next step is to present the options for how to overcome it. If you move too quickly towards a single solution people become suspicious or don't trust that you've done enough thinking. Instead, if you can lay out a range of different approaches or ideas for how to solve the pain point that you highlighted. The audience get to go on the journey with you, evaluating the pros and cons. Once again, it's important that you don't offer too many options at this point otherwise you run the risk of confusing your audience. In a sales context it could be about helping prospective customers dismiss other solutions that might be available. In an update context you could use this section to talk through attempted solutions that have failed. Whatever situation you apply the formula to, your job is to lead your audience towards the logical conclusion you are about to deliver.

Proposal

It's time to lay your cards on the table. What are you advocating for? What is your recommendation? What steps do you suggest your audience take as a result of listening to you? You're going to restate this 'call to action' in its simplest form in the *resolution* later on – that final 10% of the presentation – but this is where you need to really make the case for what you're proposing. What evidence do you have to back up your suggestion? What can people expect if they follow the path you prescribe? If you're pitching, this is where you go full out to sell the features and benefits of your product or service. Even if the goal of your presentation is a gentler form of persuasion, you still need to back up your conclusion. By the time you finish this section your audience should be in absolutely no doubt of what you are asking of them.

The POP formula allows you to build to a crescendo, logically making the case for your eventual proposal. You should support your argument in whatever ways you think will resonate most with your audience. It could be data, stories, case studies or even anecdotes. What's important is that what you choose to include reinforces both what you want your audience to *know* (the headline and key messages you identified earlier on) and what you want your audience to *do* (the call to action that you decided on).

Past – Present – Future (PPF)

Sometimes the best way to make your case is to wrap everything up into a story and that's exactly what Past – Present – Future, or PPF, helps you to achieve. This formula utilizes a tried and tested approach to storytelling to take your audience on a journey through time, helping them to engage imaginatively with the ideas you are sharing. The chronology is important here to ensure the audience doesn't get confused. We want them to move with us through the narrative step by step. Let's look at each part in turn.

Past

Start by taking people back to the beginning. If you're pitching a new idea, paint a picture of how things used to be done. If you're talking about your teams' achievements, rewind to the state of play before this project commenced. If you're telling the origin story of the organization, when did the founder have their bright idea? Your job here is to paint a picture of how things used to be, of how far we've come, of how challenging the environment was. Great stories require contrast. If the journey between the 'bad old days' and the 'brave new world' is too small or simple, the narrative loses its edge. It's important to spend sufficient time here so that the audience really understand the context. Remember that as the expert being asked to present, you're normally incredibly familiar with the background. You've lived it and breathed it, but your audience hasn't. Make sure they have a vivid image of the past reality in their minds before you move on.

Present

Now it's time to anchor your audience in the current reality. In a pitch context what is the opportunity that exists today? In a team update, you might talk about the existing status of the project. If you're in origin story mode, what does the organization look like right now? This section is all about grounding your audience in the present and helping them get a clear picture of the existing lie of the land. Great storytellers engage the senses, so move beyond facts and try to give your audience a full experience of the current reality. Engage their imaginations as well as the logical parts of their brains.

Future

Finally give your audience a vision of what is to come. For your sales pitch, what will life be like if they use your product or service? In the team meeting, what are the next milestone you are expecting to achieve? When delivering the origin story, what is the future vision of the business? The time scale here is completely context specific. You may want the audience to envisage what will be happening in two weeks' time, or how things will look two months or even two years from now. The objective is to get the people listening and to picture the version of the future you are painting in their mind. As the human brain struggles to differentiate between what is real and what is imagined, if you can help your audience to take this leap, they are already a massive step closer to the future you are describing.

The PPF formula is an extremely versatile storytelling framework and works brilliantly as a *1.2.3.* structure for the middle section of any pitch or presentation. It allows you to create a clear and compelling narrative that is easy for your audience to follow and engage with. How long you spend in each section will depend on the focus of the pitch or presentation so make sure you put yourself in your audience's shoes to determine which parts of the story are most important and help the narrative flow. There will always be elements that don't make the cut. When in doubt always err on the side of simplicity.

POP and PPF are both brilliant multi-purpose *1.2.3.* structures for the middle section. For situations where a more specific and tailored approach is required don't forget to explore Appendix A.

Remember that the suggested structures here are just that. Suggested. There are myriad ways to arrange the middle of your presentation. Just bear in mind that to make it as effective as possible, it needs to have a logical flow. That's why *1.2.3.* structures work. Keep your eyes peeled and you'll notice them everywhere. Start collecting them and as you get more familiar with the cut-through methodology I encourage you to create your own. If you do, you'll develop a repertoire you can draw on whenever you need to present.

Before we move on to how to wrap things up, a quick word on storytelling.

• •

 To download a cheat sheet of the POP and PPF
formulas for your *1.2.3.* middle as well
as the ten additional formulas found in
Appendix A visit www.cut-throughbook.com.

• •

Become a master storyteller

I've used the word narrative throughout this book but many
people feel that great storytelling is beyond their grasp. They
worry that they're too analytical or not creative enough. If this
thought process applies to you, I'd encourage you to challenge
it. Stories are all around us and we tell them all the time. We use
stories when we explain how our weekend went, when we describe
a challenging project at work or when we recount a conversation
that made us laugh. Even a sentence like 'You'll never guess what
happened this afternoon...' is the beginning of a story.

Our aim in a pitch or presentation context is not to be a grand
raconteur, spouting stories for stories' sake. Instead, we want to
use simple narrative techniques to help our audience better
understand our ideas. Stop thinking fairytale. Start thinking news
report.

As discussed, we can use Past – Present – Future (PPF) as our middle
section *1.2.3.* to turn the whole presentation into a story but even
if we take a more factual approach to proceedings, storytelling still
has a place. Human beings are hard-wired for it. It is how we've
survived and grown as a species. When we hear someone telling a
story our bodies produce oxytocin, the social bonding hormone,
literally connecting us with the person we are listening to. If you
can find a strategic way to incorporate it into your presentation it
will pay dividends in terms of audience engagement and retention
of ideas.

In all great stories, whether they're novels, films or plays there
are always sub-plots, branches off the main narrative, that have

their own beginning, middle and end. In a presentation context, there are our case studies, real-world examples, or client use cases. They're what illustrate our key messages and bring what we're staying to life. They are a powerful way to shape our content and something I would encourage you to incorporate into every presentation if you can, no matter what *1.2.3.* structure you choose. By all means give us the facts and the figures but then give us a human example that brings the numbers to life. If you collected some possible examples of this presentation stardust during the DISTLL phase, now's the time to start giving them structure and crafting something memorable for your audience.

The Past – Present – Future structure we've already discussed can definitely apply as a storytelling structure for 'sub-plots' too and is well worth considering. My two other favourites are SELL – for more personal storytelling – and SOLVE – for more data-driven narratives. Let's explore how they work.

Setting – Event – Link – Learning (SELL)

Setting

Always start by giving the story context. Paint the scene for your audience. What did it look like? Feel like? Sound like? Taste like? Smell like? Your job here is to engage their senses to help them make an imaginative leap. It's worth investing time here rather than glossing over it as so many people do. Really bring the scenario to life before you move on to the next step.

Event

This is the crossroads or the climax of the story that your whole narrative builds towards. It could be a moment of struggle, a key realization, the point that everything suddenly falls into place or when it all completely fell apart. It is the highest emotional point in your story, the peak of the action, that everything else leads to.

Link

Now it's time to make it personal and reveal how you felt or how the story impacted those involved. Draw out the emotion that the event created. If you're telling a personal story you should use 'I felt..' here to accentuate the resonance. If you're telling someone else's story, how did they feel at this point? What was the emotional journey that took place?

Learning

In a business context there must be a point to every story you tell. A 'so what' that you share with the audience. What is the moral of the story? What did you learn from the experience? Why are you sharing it with your audience? Make it explicit so that your audience has their own 'ah-ha' moment.

The SELL formula is great for stories where you were personally at the heart of the action, but it can also be used to showcase someone else's experience. It focuses on human connection, emotion and meaning, engaging listeners with clear tangible takeaways.

Situation – Obstacle – Logic – Victory – Evidence (SOLVE)

Situation

Again, context is key but this time the focus is more around the initial challenge or need. What is the starting point for the narrative? Give the background. Who or what was involved and why was it important?

Obstacle

Now talk about what got in the way. What was the big roadblock or difficulty? Give details of the constraints or challenges. You need to help the audience understand why the problem couldn't initially be solved. What was missing? What was the impact of the problem on those involved?

Logic

This is the part of the story where the thinking changed. What logical steps were taken? What approach, tool or insight helped to overcome the obstacle? What was the solution being developed? Who was involved and what role did they play? What were the critical choices and decisions that moved the needle?

Victory

This is the breakthrough. The moment that the obstacle is finally overcome. How did it happen? How did it feel? How did others react? What were the knock-on effects? Show how the effort and strategy led to success.

Evidence

How do you know that it worked? What key takeaways or lessons were revealed? How has or can the solution be sustained, expanded or replicated? Are there any direct quotes, testimonials or data points that validate the success? This section is about demonstrating that 'they all lived happily ever after'!

The SOLVE formula is perfect for case-studies, business cases and data driven stories. It is process focused and solution driven, helping the audience understand the nuance behind a logical argument.

Both SELL and SOLVE can be used in a variety of different situations and are a great way to bring your argument to life in the hearts and minds of the audience. They help to make case studies and examples more tangible and will make your overall message more 'sticky'. It is, however, important that storytelling builds your overall narrative rather than detracts from it, so it's worth bearing in mind the following:

1. Keep things short and punchy. These are sub-plots, not the main event. Use them to spice up your message but don't let them overpower it.

2. Make sure you focus on the emotional connection. Most of us find the logic part much easier so don't be afraid to accentuate the feelings in the story.

3. Show, don't tell. Be specific and detailed in your story-telling. The more vivid your description the easier it is for your audience to imagine what you are saying.

4. And finally, be wary of making yourself the hero. I'm not saying you, your company, product or service can't ever be the star of the show but it's actually much more effective to make the audience (or some like them) the centre of attention. In his brilliant book *Building a Story Brand*, Donald Miller says 'When we position our customer as the hero and ourselves as the guide, we will be recognized as a trusted resource to help them overcome their challenges'.[2] It's sage advice and it doesn't just apply to customers. The same can be said for all stakeholders, internal and external. People love it when they can imagine themselves as the hero of the story.

Now that you've sorted your storytelling, and you can see how it forms an important part of your *1.2.3.* middle section, it's time so move your focus to how to finish with a bang.

• •

 To download a cheat sheet of the SELL and SOLVE formulas for storytelling visit www.cut-throughbook.com.

• •

 STAND & DELIVER

• •

CHOOSE YOUR MIDDLE *1.2.3.*

It's time to decide on the most appropriate *1.2.3.* for your middle section. Which of the three-part structures works best to bring your message to life? Don't forget to think about 'the audience' and 'the goal' as these will influence the framework that you choose.

Once you've decided on the structure, map out what you will include in each of the three sections. Ensure that there is a logical flow. Are there any SELL or SOLVE stories you want to include to illustrate your points? You can of course script in full, but I recommend starting with bullet points at this stage. You need to ensure that everything fits together before you get into the finer detail.

Also give some thought as to how much time you want to allocate to each of the three sections. The aim isn't necessarily to make them equal but deciding upfront will ensure that you aren't spending too long in the wrong part of the narrative.

Once you've got a bullet point plan decide on whether you now want to more formally script some of the sections or whether a looser framework will suffice. If in doubt, keep things to high-level talking points as this gives you much more flexibility when it comes to delivering the final pitch or presentation.

• •

Excellent endings

Often the close is a last-minute thought. We spend so much time worrying about the opening and the middle section that by the time we get to the end of the pitch or presentation we are just hoping for the best. This is a lousy strategy! Your ending plays such a significant part in influencing your audience that it can't be an afterthought. If we go back to our 20:70:10 ratio we have roughly 10% of our total time to bring everything together so we want to be economical and impactful with how we conclude.

In *Thinking, Fast and Slow*, Nobel Prize winner Daniel Kahneman introduces readers to 'The Peak End Rule'.[3] Essentially our lasting memory of an experience is dictated by a combination of the emotional peak of that experience and its final moments.

That means you can be brilliant throughout your presentation but if you finish poorly your impact will be disproportionally diminished. It's therefore vital that we finish strong.

Before I give you the formula to help you go out with a bang, we should first spend some time on what to avoid. There are three key mistakes that I often see people making. The first is letting things fall off a cliff. You're progressing along nicely, your audience is engaged, when all of a sudden, things come to an abrupt and unexpected end. This is really jarring for the audience and means that their final focus is on the last topic you covered rather than a proper conclusion where all the threads are synthesized together. It almost feels like the person presenting has forgotten what's coming next and has frozen in mid flow.

The second mistake is the fade to black. This is where things just seem to inexplicably fizzle out. This is normally accompanied by a decrease in energy or volume and a series of 'umms' and 'errs'. Just like a pop song that doesn't have an ending and just fades out, there is no definite conclusion to proceedings, leaving your audience with a feeling of uncertainty around the point of your message. The presenter just runs out of steam and any previous impact is lost.

The final mistake is death by Q&A. Your content is great, you bring things together with a nice conclusion and then you ask your audience for their thoughts. This is a risky approach! I'll cover how to prepare for questions later in the book but it's important that your pitch or presentation doesn't end with you handing over control to your audience. The danger here is that the questions asked pull everyone in a different direction so that the final thing that people remember is something completely 'off message'.

Instead, what I suggest you do is invite questions throughout the presentation, as this gives you more scope to finish powerfully on your own terms. If the organizer or client insists on finishing with Q&A, then the best approach is to deliver your conclusion, open things up for questions and then ensure that you make time right at the end to redeliver a micro version of the conclusion so that you have control of the final narrative.

To avoid the pitfalls mentioned above there is a simple four-step process I suggest you follow that will allow you to wrap up any presentation in a memorable and impactful way. The acronym to use is *S.A.L.T.*

- ▶ **S**ummarize
- ▶ **A**sk
- ▶ **L**ink
- ▶ **T**hank

Summarize

Your ending should start with a summary of the key ideas that your pitch or presentation has dealt with. You will have a covered a lot of ground over the course of your narrative, so now is the time to bring everything together. During the DISTIL phase you decided on three to five key messages that hopefully have been peppered throughout. Now is the time to reiterate them. There are no prizes for subtlety at this stage, your job is to make sure that the audience walks away with the important things front and centre in their minds. Be bold and deliberate in telling listeners what you want them to remember.

Ask

Next you need to give your audience a clear 'call to action'. Hopefully this has been seeded throughout the presentation so what you're asking for or recommending shouldn't come out of the blue. However, it is important that this request is ringing in their ears as you wrap things up. Again, we identified this call to action in the DISTIL phase and now is the time to spell it out in its simplest terms. If you want your team to do things differently, tell them. If you'd like your audience to spread the word, ask them. If you would love to work with the prospect, say so. This section of the close should leave the audience in no doubt as to what you are asking them to do.

Link

The human brain looks for order. Loose ends can be incredibly distracting. A brilliant way to signal to your audience that you are wrapping up is to close a loop. Find a way to echo or reference something you said at the beginning, so that the presentation goes full circle. This is a narrative device we're very used to in the movies. We see the hero return to where they started as a better, wiser version of themselves. If you look out for it, you'll often see accomplished speakers closing their presentations by concluding a story that they began earlier on. When you take people back to a key idea or concept that you introduced near the beginning of the presentation you give them an unconscious feeling of closure. It's a really satisfying experience for the audience and helps them focus on the 'summary' and 'ask' you've just delivered, rather than searching for any incomplete threads in your argument.

Thank

Finally, we mustn't forget to say thank you. Finish with gratitude for your audience and the attention they have given you. In any presentation it's all about them, not about you, so we need to acknowledge the time they have invested with us. It is obviously a common courtesy but, done with authenticity, it also creates a powerful bond between you and your listeners. The simple act of saying 'thank you' also leaves your audience in no doubt that you have finished, marking a definite end to the presentation. Do it well, and in certain contexts it may even trigger a round of applause!

Summarize what you've told them, make your ask, link back to the beginning and finish with a thank you (*S.A.L.T.*).

These four steps will allow you to conclude any presentation with confidence and authority. Don't leave the lasting impression you create for your audience up to chance. Instead, use the *S.A.L.T.* formula to take control of the narrative and finish on a high.

Now you've got your *S.A.L.T.* structure, it's worth taking a moment to zoom back out to the big picture.

STAND & DELIVER

• •

SEASON YOUR ENDING WITH *S.A.L.T.*

Start to sketch out your ending using the *S.A.L.T.* acronym. Again, we don't need to script things in full, we need to get a shape that we can work with and refine. The questions below will aid your thinking.

Summarize

What are the ideas, topics or themes you have covered? If your audience only remembers three to five things from your presentation, what should they be? Is there a logical order or sequence in which to present these ideas?

Ask

What is your 'call to action'? What do you want your audience to do as a result of listening to you? If there aren't practical steps for your audience to take, what should they be thinking about or considering as a result of hearing you speak?

Link

Is there an obvious loop that you open at the beginning that you close at the end? Is there a key theme or idea that you could refer back to? Is there a story that you could return to and conclude? How can you reassure your audience that all loose ends have been tied up?

Thank

Who do you need to say thank you to? (Hint: it's the people who have been listening!)

Calculate roughly how long you have for this final part of the presentation. We're working on the assumption that you will spend 10% or less of your total time here. How does this impact the way you deliver the close? You may only have time for a sentence or two to cover each step. If you have more time to play with, decide how you want to allocate it across the four parts of the *S.A.L.T.* ending.

To download a worksheet of these questions to help you craft your *S.A.L.T.* ending visit www.cut-throughbook.com.

A presentation on a page

As we've explored so far in this book there are many important elements to consider when designing a successful presentation. It can seem overwhelming but it's actually a logical process. We just need to follow the steps in the right order. Figure 6 is a template for a 'presentation on a page'. It brings together all the elements we have discussed so far to help you see a complete snapshot of your structure. If you respond to each of the questions or prompts with a couple of words you will have the basis for an outstanding pitch or presentation. You can then use this as a roadmap to help you build out your script and any visual elements you plan to use. If you're time poor, you can also use this 'presentation on page' without any additional material to deliver an impactful narrative.

Now you've got your structure sorted, it's finally time to give some thought to what you use to bring the message to life.

To download an A4 or A3 template of a 'presentation on a page' that includes space for you to fill in your answers to the questions, visit www.cut-throughbook.com.

❶ → THE EXAM QUESTION

- What question does this pitch or presentation answer for the audience?

❷ → THE AUDIENCE

- Who is the audience?
- Facts
- Feelings
- In Flow Energy Centres: Head, Heart, Gut, Feet

❸ → THE GOAL

- Is this a 'feature film' or 'box set'?
- What outcome am I looking for?

❹ → THE COMPETITION

- Define – who or what am I competing with?
- Differentiate – what will make me stand out?
- Destory – how can I build a case against them?

❺ → KNOW

- What is my headline?
- What are my three key messages?

❻ → FEEL

- What is the emotional journey I want to take my audience on?
- How do I want them to feel at the end?

❼ → DO

- What is my call to action?
- What is the logical next step I want the audience to take?

❽ → NOW

- Why is now the time for action?
- Am I moving the audience 'towards' a solution or 'away from' a problem?

❾ → STARDUST

- What are some of the memorable elements I will use?
- Facts and Figures?
- Case-studies and Stories?
- Visuals?
- Testimonials and Social Proof?
- Metaphor and Simile?

❿ → S.T.A.R.

- What is my S.T.A.R. opening?
- Surprise
- Takeaways
- Authority
- Roadmap

20%

⓫ → 1.2.3. MIDDLE

- Which 1.2.3. formula should I use for the middle section?
- Problems – Options – Proposal?
- Past – Present – Future?
- Which 'Stardust' elements should I include here?

70%

⓬ → S.A.L.T.

- What is my S.A.L.T. close?
- Summarize
- Ask
- Link
- Thank

10%

Figure 6 A presentation on a page

Choose your visual approach

You now know what you're going to say, but how are you going to help your audience visualize it? There will of course be instances where your presentation requires nothing more than you standing up in front of your audience or looking down the lens of the camera. Great orators through the ages have powerfully engaged their audiences without the need for slides or props but that doesn't necessarily mean you should go without.

As you know by now, I'm all for simplicity, so if your message can be delivered without any support, go for it! You'll need to be well prepared and rehearsed but this minimalist approach is seriously impressive when done well and oozes confidence to an audience. However, often you'll really benefit from using something in addition to your words to reinforce your key ideas.

The obvious approach is to reach for the slide deck, and this can work brilliantly as long as you do it right. If your pitch or presentation is technical, some well-designed graphs or visuals can go a long way to illustrate your point. If you're telling more of a story, striking images will help bring things to life. We'll look at best practices for this shortly.

However, you shouldn't be afraid to think outside the box. A well-chosen prop can really help to make your message 'sticky'. We're not talking grabbing a random item from your desk to hold on to as a comfort blanket. Instead, ask yourself if there's anything specific that could help you viscerally illustrate your point. Bill Gates' TED talk[4] on malaria made a vivid impression on his audience because of the power of his prop. If you haven't seen it, I highly recommend you search it out.

Another hybrid option that works well especially in a pitch context is a 'placemat'. This is usually an A3 size handout printed on both sides with key information. This replaces the slide deck and you direct your audience to the relevant sections as you build your narrative. As with any visual aid, great design is important here. You must keep it simple enough that it doesn't become a distraction but also detailed enough that it is a valuable addition to what you are saying.

If in doubt I suggest sticking to a well-designed slide deck to support your message, so let's explore the dos and don'ts.

Don't kill them with boring slides

Most of us have experienced death by PowerPoint at some point in our lives. There's nothing worse than sitting in a room watching someone read something off the screen that you have already read yourself. And yet many people are still guilty of replicating this dreadful experience for their own audiences. Splitting your script into five bullet points, dumping them onto a slide in size eight font and then reciting those bullet points verbatim is not presenting, it's reading. Don't do it! If you want to pitch and present like the best, you have to raise your game.

If you've been following the process I've laid out so far, rather than a duplicated version of your last presentation, hopefully you've either got a brain dump of slide ideas or a blank document in front of you. Your job now is to build a clear and compelling visual narrative that supports and enhances your message, rather than detracts from it.

I could write a whole other book on slide design alone but Garr Reynolds' *Presentation Zen Design*[5] and Lee Jackson's *Get Good at Slides*[6] are both so good that I've decided to leave it up to them. If you don't have time to read either, here are some important principles to consider.

1. Your slides are not your script

Let's be clear. Your slides are not there for you to read from. They're there to help your audience engage with and retain your message. If you feel like you want to use your deck as an aide-memoire, it's a good indication that you've got it wrong. A well-constructed slide deck can actually really help you navigate your message, with each new slide becoming a prompt for what you want to say next. But the only time you should ever be reading from the screen is if there is a quote that you are sharing which you want to speak accurately. At all other times I'd encourage you to think of it as 'set dressing'. If it wasn't there (and at some point in your life, when the tech fails unexpectedly, it won't be) you should still be able to deliver the message in a way that resonates with your audience.

2. We don't know your data as well as you do

The phrase I hear that makes me most angry in a pitch or presentation is 'As you can see from the slide'. In 99.999% of instances, what's on the screen in front of me is some complex piece of information that I'm seeing for the very first time. At that point I want to jump to my feet and shout at the presenter 'I can't see anything. It's your slide!'. It's too easy to assume that just because the data or information we are sharing is obvious to us, it will also be obvious to those we are sharing it with. We forget that often we've been looking at this information for ages. It's our area of expertise and compared to our audience we know it inside out and back to front.

If you want people to go with you, you must provide context. You need to orientate them to what they're seeing. If you're sharing a graph, don't just show people the whole thing. Build it up. Start with the axis and the key. Set the scene. Tell people that you're going to be illustrating and then build it line by line in front of them. Any slide software you use will enable you to do this with a few clicks and it will transform your presentations. Sharing data in this way takes a few seconds more but it ensures that your audience is focusing on what you are telling them, not zoning out to try to draw their own conclusions whilst you continue to speak.

3. If you include it, include it deliberately

If you don't intend to use a slide, take it out of the deck or put it in the appendix. If you flick past slides without explaining them, you risk your audience feeling like they're missing out. Likewise phrases like 'I know you can't really see it but…' or 'I know this slide is really busy, however…' can unconsciously make your audience feel undervalued. It can feel like you couldn't be bothered to put in the work, which I'm sure isn't true, so it's not a risk worth taking.

Any visuals you use should be designed specifically for your audience with the express purpose of helping them to understand your message. If what you have created is difficult to understand, too small to read properly or requires your audience to ignore part of it in order to make your point, you need to go back to the drawing board. It's helpful to think of visuals in a binary way. They either add to the message (in which case they stay) or they subtract from it (in which case they go). There's no space for neutral in a winning presentation.

4. Less is not always more

Somewhere over the last decade a myth has developed that needs to be busted. People often tell me that they've been told they should never have more than ten slides. Why? If you need ten slides or less to deliver your message, great. But less is not always more. Trying to limit the number of slides often encourages people to pack each one with multiple ideas in a tiny font. My advice is to use as may slides as you need to share your message clearly and impactfully.

Each slide should articulate a single idea. If you're comparing two things side-by-side there's an argument for them appearing together. If not, it's best to put them on a new page. I remember turning up to deliver a speech at a conference and seeing the panic on the organizer's face when they realized that I had a 67-page deck for my 45-minute slot. They were petrified my talk would last hours. Instead, it came in at 44 minutes and 32 seconds. My slides were deliberately chosen to illustrate each of the ideas I was talking about and I was using them at a rate of roughly one and half slides a minute to keep the presentation flowing and engaging.

I'm not going to prescribe a number of slides per minute of presentation. Instead, I'd simply encourage you to give your ideas space to breathe and your audience space to digest them.

5. It needs to pass the mobile phone test

As Lee Jackson says 'Bullets don't just kill people, they kill presentations too'.[7] Far too many slide decks, especially in the corporate world contain far, far too many words. Again, I'm not going to dictate the number of words per page, the font size or how many bullet points you do or don't use. But I am going to ask you to be honest with yourself. When you're in the audience, if there's text on the screen do you try to read it? Ninety-nine percent of people will answer 'yes'. Given that reality, now consider this question: When you're reading the text on the screen are you able to give the presenter your full attention? Ninety-nine percent of people will answer 'no'.

If you read and don't listen when others are showing you words on the screen, why will your audience be any different? For clarity, they won't. We therefore need to simplify our visual content. A good benchmark is what I call 'the mobile phone test'. If your audience was dialling into your presentation on their mobile phone and walking down the street holding it in portrait, would they still be able to read your visuals? In the world of virtual meetings this scenario is not as far-fetched as it might seem. If you design with 'the mobile phone test' in mind, no matter whether you're presenting to a 1,000 seat auditorium or a group of investors on Zoom, everyone will be able to see what you're talking about.

6. Your presentation deck might not be their takeaway deck

We've already established that your slides are not your script but they're also not a brochure or a complete and comprehensive record of exactly what you said either. A presentation deck and a takeaway deck serve two different purposes and shouldn't be confused. The presentation deck helps you bring your argument to life at a big picture level. The takeaway deck goes into the detail.

If you need both, the easiest thing to do is to create the takeaway deck first, ensuring that it follows your presentation narrative, and then start to delete stuff. Turn single pages with multiple graphs into multiple slides with single graphs. Delete all the verbiage that you absolutely want people to read in the takeaway deck but absolutely don't want them to read in the presentation deck. Depending on the audience and the context you may even want to add visual 'stickers' to the presentation deck referencing where people can find the more detailed version of the information in the takeaway deck. The two documents, if you need both, should be completely complimentary but completely different.

Slide design is a skill worth honing. Done well it will benefit you and your audience. If you use the principles above, you will create a visual narrative that helps you reinforce your key messages and makes your presentation much more memorable and 'sticky', allowing your message to cut through.

 I've shared the principles above in the clearest way I could in words on a page but sometimes there's no substitute for seeing things. With that in mind, I've created a video walking you through, in detail, the six principles for slide design. You can watch it at www.cut-throughbook.com.

 STAND & DELIVER

MAKE SURE IT FLOWS

Great presentations flow. Poor presentations are lumpy. Now that you've got a S.T.A.R. opening, a 1.2.3. middle and a S.A.L.T. close, it's time to make sure it all fits together seamlessly. Open your script outline document or your slide deck. Put yourself in your audience's shoes and then consider the following questions:

- Is there a clear 'so what?' for each section and slide?

- Is all the information shared relevant to the audience?

- If you just read the titles or headline text on each slide, would the narrative make sense?

- If there is no text, are the images used compelling and memorable?

- Is there a clear linear structure that is easy to follow?

- Are the key messages clear and reinforced throughout?

- Is the narrative engaging, without moments that feel repetitive or jarring?

If the answer to all the above is 'yes', you're ready to start rehearsing. If there is one or more 'no', take some time to address the issues before you move on.

• •

Chapter summary

The third step of this playbook is a bit of an epic one. You've taken all your initial thinking and wrestled it into a structure that will help you bring your key messages to life. The frameworks I have shared are designed to support you, but you shouldn't be a slave to them. Tweak and adapt where necessary with a singular focus of crafting a presentation that speaks directly to your audience.

By the end of this phase, you should have created the following:

✓ A *S.T.A.R.* opening to help you grab your audience's attention from the outset

✓ A *1.2.3.* middle structure tailored to your context and goal

✓ A *S.A.L.T.* close to wrap your presentation with impact

✓ Props or a slide deck that will support you in delivering your message and make it 'stickier' for your audience.

This step is quite labour intensive and requires you to commit to your ideas. You can of course tweak things, making additions and subtractions as you move into the DRILL phase but the stronger the foundations you lay at this stage, the easier it is to focus on your delivery and how you bring the words to life.

If you can, it's also worth bringing in other people at the end of this stage to offer you feedback. Is the messaging clear? Do the visuals support your narrative? The more you can sense check your approach now, the fewer last-minute changes you'll be making later.

If you're happy with the structure, it's time to talk about rehearsal.

Chapter four

DRILL: Prepare a star performance

Step 4: Drill

Great pitches and presentations evolve. They don't start life fully formed. It doesn't matter how wonderful the ideas are, how stunning the visuals are or how clever your script is. If it's not delivered brilliantly, it will fall flat. Before you can deliver an amazing performance, however, you need to put in the work behind the scenes. That's why DRILL is Step 4 of the playbook. You have to fail in private in order to succeed in public.

This is a step that many people resist, either because of a perceived lack of time or a fear of looking silly. They think they can get away with reading things through a couple of times or running the lines in their heads. Unless you are an exceptionally talented improvisor, this is invariably a recipe for disaster.

Instead, I'd encourage you to embrace the uncomfortableness of this stage. I promise you it's where the magic really happens. When you properly practise what you're going to say and how you're going to say it, you suddenly see where the holes and the weak links are. You get a feel for what works and what doesn't. If you've laid the foundations in the steps before there shouldn't be massive changes. But the tweaks you make will be the difference between winning and losing, between that smiling round of applause or the stony-faced reception of your audience.

I'm here to tell you that you can't skip the hard work. But you can make it as efficient and effective as possible. Let's look at how.

Rehearse like a pro

Over the last couple of decades working with people in business, I've heard every excuse under the sun as to why people don't properly rehearse. The most prevalent is that 'it makes me too wooden'. My reply to this is 'you just haven't rehearsed enough!'.

Let me take you back to my former profession of acting. When I was involved in a theatre production, the average rehearsal period was between four and six weeks. To get a two-hour show ready for an audience, the cast were spending 20 to 30 days in the rehearsal room, from 9am until 5pm. And that's not counting the private line-learning or the multiple days of technical and dress rehearsal that happened once you got into the theatre. Somewhere between 140 and 210 hours in the rehearsal room for a two-hour presentation.

To be clear, I'm not suggesting that the next time you're asked to present you block out two full weeks in your calendar. But I would ask you to reflect honestly on whether your current average rehearsal allocation is enough to set yourself up for success. Actors would never dream of picking up a script, reading it a couple of times in their heads and then stepping in front of an audience. Neither should you.

The process of getting so familiar with your narrative and your ideas that you can speak the words 'as if for the first time' is labour intensive. If you're coming across as wooden it's because you don't know it well enough yet. As I've said already, I really don't suggest you script every line. If you do, you have to work even harder to really own the words. But even when you're working with a series of bullet point ideas for each section of your presentation, you need to know things inside out and back to front. The words you use each time might differ slightly, but you need to have a clear idea of what's coming next.

I appreciate that sometimes it's difficult to find sufficient time alongside all your other work and life tasks to rehearse. I also appreciate that if you're delivering as part of a team things become even more complex. So, what I'd like to offer is a guide to what I would class as best practice and some thoughts on your minimal viable rehearsal (MVR) if you have no alternative.

The first thing to get through is what I lovingly call the 'the car crash'. Most people resist starting the process of drilling their presentation because they're worried that they'll mess it up. They want to avoid getting egg on their face in front of their colleagues.

Or if they're rehearsing alone, they want every word that comes out of their mouth to be perfect. To offer some words of reassurance, this is *never* going to happen. No matter how much preparation you do, the first time you speak your words aloud it's likely to be a mess. And that's fine. In fact, that's perfect. It's exactly the point of the first rehearsal. You're going to forget things. You're going to trip over your words. You're going to click the wrong slide at the wrong time. But it's much more preferable that you do this in the safety of the rehearsal room than in front of your actual audience. Get 'the car crash' out of the way early so that the real work can begin.

The next stage of the process is what I think of as 'private rehearsal'. This happens behind closed doors. If you're working as a team, your teammates can be in the room but you're not seeking external feedback. This is where you develop familiarity, where you get a sense of the flow and an understanding of how everything fits together. You may well make tweaks as you go. This part of the process can still be messy but with 'the car crash' over and done with, you can place more focus on how to improve things rather than just getting though them. If the pitch or presentation is quite lengthy it can be useful to split it into sections and spend blocks of time working in isolation before you put the whole thing back together.

Once you're happy with how things are working, it's time for a sense check. This is where you move into 'public rehearsal'. You might invite colleagues or friends to watch, or you might bring in a coach. The objective of this phase is to test things in front of an audience. It can still be stop-start at this point, but you need to be clear with your audience about what you are looking for. Brief them well and be specific about the feedback you're seeking. Do you want to stress-test the structure? Do you want them to focus on the visuals? What elements of your performance do you want them to critique? If your pitch or presentation will include questions from the audience, this is the point in the rehearsal process to start introducing them too.

The penultimate rehearsal phase is the 'technical rehearsal'. Just like preparing for a theatre show there comes a point where things are ready to go in front of an audience (or you've just run out of time!). However, there's a difference between the rehearsal room and your performance space and you need to bridge the gap. You may have been rehearsing virtually, or in a room that's completely different from the one you'll be delivering the final presentation in. Whilst you may not be able to get into the actual performance space, I'd suggest you replicate things as much as possible and keep your focus on the technical elements. Will you be seated or standing? Where will you be in relation to the screen? If you're delivering virtually, how will you share the slides? If you're presenting as a team, who does what and when? Dedicate a whole rehearsal session to these purely technical elements to ensure you have ironed out any issues.

Finally, it's time for the 'dress rehearsal'. This should be a complete run through from beginning to end without stopping. If something goes wrong, you cover it. If you forget what's coming next, you take a deep breath and find a way through. Do what you would do if it were the real thing. You can invite an audience to this rehearsal for sure but if you ask them to engage in Q&A don't allow this to become the focus. You should have practised for any challenging questions in the 'public rehearsal' phase. This 'dress rehearsal' is about creating a muscle memory of how it feels to flow seamlessly through the presentation. A word about feedback at this stage of proceedings too. My suggestion is to keep it to a very high level at this point. It's not the time to reinvent the wheel. It's time to build confidence so that your go into the real thing feeling ready to perform at your best.

The car crash → Private rehearsal → Public rehearsal →
Technical rehearsal → Dress rehearsal

The stages above are my suggestions for an ideal rehearsal process, but we need to acknowledge that we don't live in an ideal world. If you can't carve out time for all the steps, where should you place your focus? What constitutes your MVR?

In my experience, where you'll get most return on your rehearsal investment is by working on the beginning and the end. As we've already explored, these are vital moments for getting your audience's attention and reinforcing your key messages and your call to action. Spend as much time working on them as possible.

For most people once they get past the introduction the nerves diminish, and they find their flow. Drilling your *S.T.A.R.* opening will mean that you know exactly how you're going to kick things off which will allow you to focus on connecting with your audience. Likewise working your *S.A.L.T.* close over and over will ensure that you finish strong. Be very aware how you manage your time to avoid over allocating to the beginning of the presentation. It's a natural thing to do but you risk ending on a weak note – and as we discussed with the 'peak end rule' when looking at crafting your close, that's something to avoid.

There's no right or wrong answer for how long you need to rehearse but I would encourage you to block out as much time as you possibly can. Until you've spoken the words aloud a few times it's very difficult to tell what's working and what's not. Remember too that 30 minutes of completely focused preparation is worth hours of semi-distracted time. Book a meeting room or find a quiet space and start speaking the words aloud. Failing that I've even been known to put my headphones in and walk down the street saying my lines. People just think you're on the phone! Be selfish and make sure you have the time you need to perform at your best.

Before we move on, here are a few more thoughts about scripts.

STAND & DELIVER

• •

CREATE A REHEARSAL SCHEDULE

If you're anything like me, if it's not in the diary, it doesn't happen. Make sure you take time to create a rehearsal plan. Ideally you should do this the moment you know you're delivering the pitch or presentation. Even if you don't know the exact date it's worth pencilling something in so that you have time reserved in the diary. Start with the delivery date and then work backwards:

Delivery date:

Dress rehearsal (ideally 1 before the delivery date):

Technical rehearsal (usually 1–2 days before):

Public rehearsal(s) (try to have at least 2 of these especially if there will be Q&A):

Private rehearsals (as many as you can):

The car crash (get this in as early as possible):

Once these sessions are in the diary make them non-negotiable. Even if you don't feel ready remember that rehearsal happens in your body not in your head. Sit or stand up, take a deep breath and start speaking the words.

• •

Bring the words to life

The scariest day in the rehearsal room for any actor is the day the director tells them to put down the script. At that moment, like it or not, you lose your crutch. You no longer have a safety net and must commit to the words coming out of your mouth whether they are correct or completely made up. In a business context most people never get to that day.

For an actor that day is not only scary, it is also liberating. When I push my business clients to do the same in a rehearsal context, they eventually find it liberating too. Having our notes in our hand or reading from our laptop screen may feel safe but it kills the audience connection. Think back to the last conference you attended. There will have been speakers who stood, hands gripping the lectern, reading from their script, and there were (hopefully) others who moved freely round the stage as they spoke. Who did you feel more connected with? Who seemed more engaging? Who was easier to listen to?

Unless you're a president, a prime minster or delivering a message that must be spoken word for word for compliance purposes, there are very few instances where reading from the page is necessary or advisable. If you've used the frameworks I've recommended so far, you should have a solid outline of your talking points. If, however, you went one step further and created a fuller script, your job now is to try to forget it. Instead, your focus should be on bringing your words to life.

As you practise, rather than putting all your attention on the text that you have created, go back to your emotional intentions. How do you want your audience to feel? Combine that with the thinking you have done around your key messages and the words should take care of themselves. Say them over and over, iterating and allowing them to change as you explore. Eventually you'll settle on a shape that you are happy with. You don't have to use exactly the same words every time but if you practise enough, you'll find each version becomes more and more similar. Working in this way should give you greater flexibility when it comes to the final presentation. It also ensures that it sounds authentic as for most of us, how we speak is very different from how we write.

There are a few other things worth bearing in mind as you rehearse. The first is energy. In my book, *IMPACT*, I discuss the importance of 'level 8 energy'. If you imagine a scale of 1 to 10, 1 is 'man-flu' and 10 is 'two bars of chocolate and a can of your favourite energy drink'. The performance sweet spot is 'level 8'. This is where you're leading the energy in the room but not completely overpowering things. 'Level 8' energy is also what you need for rehearsal. If you don't develop a muscle memory of how to bring your message to life for your audience, you'll have nothing to fall back on when the time to deliver it comes and you'll fail to create cut-through.

You mustn't be self-conscious of playing full out in rehearsal. If you don't go all in, you won't know whether things are working.

It's easy to hide behind phrases like 'obviously I won't do it like this on the day' or 'I'm just going to focus on the words rather than the performance' but you're doing yourself a disservice. Stand if you plan to stand. Engage with the camera if you'll be presenting virtually (more on this later). And most importantly don't forget to smile! Push the boundaries and see how much you can dial things up. Most of us are pretty bad at calibrating our own performance, so it's worth seeking feedback from others too. What may feel very over-the-top energy to us, can often come across as pitch perfect to our audience.

One of the best ways to gauge how your performance is landing is to film your rehearsal. I know that sentence will have sent shivers down many readers' spines but it's an objective way of benchmarking what you're doing. I'll be very honest and say upfront that it's unlikely to be a pleasant experience. Every now and again I see myself pop up on the television in a rerun of one of the shows I appeared in during my acting days. It makes me cringe! I can't believe I looked like that or sounded like that. But of course, I did. And when I take a deep breath and get over myself it's not as bad as I think.

With all the YouTube video content I produce these days I'm much more used to seeing myself on screen and I now relish the opportunity to get hold of the footage of a speech I've delivered as it gives me a chance to review and refine my performance. Give it a go, and once you get over the initial discomfort, I promise it will be worth it.

Doing all this on your own is one thing but if you're presenting as part of a team there are some additional elements you need to think about.

Fine tune your teamwork

Back in the DISCOVER phase we looked at picking the right team. If you decide to go down the group presentation route, rehearsals inevitably look a little bit different. The biggest hurdle is normally aligning diaries and coordinating schedules! If we take the need to rehearse as much as possible as a given, how does what happens in the room with a team differ to doing things solo?

The first thing to consider is focus. You need to optimize everyone's time. When you rehearse a play, a TV show or a film you don't have the full cast sitting around day in, day out. Apply the same principle to your rehearsals. At the beginning of the DRILL phase, it's useful to gather everyone together to set expectations and get through 'the car crash' rehearsal but after that, divide and conquer. Are there sections that you can work on independently or in small groups?

Be strategic about the time you spend together. Working from the beginning of the presentation to the end, over and over will get you a mediocre result. Break things down into sections and then build things up. Actors rehearse one scene at a time and then start joining the scenes together into Acts before joining the Acts together in a full run-through. This is an ideal approach. If you can, it's worth having someone who's not actually delivering the pitch to act as the 'runner' organizing and coordinating the rehearsals and making sure that things are on track. The 'runner' can also ensure that all sections of the pitch or presentation are getting adequate rehearsal so that there are no weak links.

One area to focus on when drilling a group presentation is the introduction. The *S.T.A.R.* opening is still great in this context, but you'll need to fit multiple personal intros into the 'authority' section. It's important in any group delivery that everyone gets a voice early on. If there are people on the team who don't say anything until near the end of the presentation, their status is greatly diminished by the time they open their mouths, so each team member's introduction is vital to give them the right to be in the room. You may also be introducing the wider organization to your audience at this point, so timing here is important. Make sure everyone has an opportunity to speak about themselves and highlight something about their experience that is relevant to the topic and the audience. You need to come across as a team of experts. If you can, also factor in other chances to rotate who is speaking during the first half of the presentation so no team member spends too long in silence.

When working as a team some of the most important moments are actually the transitions between speakers. These can easily be missed in the 'private rehearsal' phase especially if people are practising independently. However, these seemingly insignificant interactions have a huge impact on how the team as a whole is perceived. You often hear 'poor team dynamic' cited as a reason for losing a pitch. These in-between moments are where trust and confidence are demonstrated.

Think of it like a 4 x 100m relay race. Each individual sprinter can be at the top of the game but if they drop the baton at the handover, the team are almost certain to lose. The same is true in pitches and presentations. If the energy drops off a cliff between speakers or if people are talking over each other and metaphorically wrestling for the mic, alarm bells start ringing for the audience. Decide between you how you will know that each section is over. A foolproof way to do it is simply to say your co-presenter's name and something like 'over to you', when you're done with your sections. There are of course much more elegant ways to do things. The important thing is that everyone is on the same page and trusts the process. It's worth getting feedback on the transitions from an audience member during the 'public rehearsal' phase to sense-check how things are working.

In a similar vein, working out who's driving the tech – if you're using slides – is an important consideration in team presentations. If you're standing up, will you pass the clicker between you? If not, how can you prime your team mates to know when to advance things on screen? The words 'next slide please' have a real ability to kill the flow for an audience, so avoid them if you can. If you're seated around a table, I'd recommend one person is in charge of the deck. If this is the case, you'll need to practise at length together to ensure you get the timing right. These may seem like insignificant details but they're the difference between a great team performance and an average one!

Finally, a word on listening. As part of the rehearsal process you need to get used to listening to your teammates. When you're not speaking it's your job to direct the audience's attention. You do this by looking at the speaker and being present to what they are saying. You don't need to fixate on them exclusively. You'll naturally want to move your attention to the audience from time to time to check in with them. But when you show interest in what your colleagues are saying – rather than staring at your notes or looking off into the middle distance – you unconsciously signal to your audience that something of value is being shared. Look at any great TV presenting duo and it's exactly what they do. They give each other attention and focus. Make sure you build this into your rehearsal process, otherwise you'll forget to do it on the day.

If your presentation is virtual or hybrid there are a couple of other things you need to consider at this stage too.

 STAND & DELIVER

• •

SPEED RUNS

Whether you're rehearsing as a team or alone there's another tool from the world of acting that can come in handy, especially if you're time poor. It's called a 'speed run' and it does what it says on the tin. Actors use speed runs at the very end of the rehearsal practice to see how well they know the lines, speaking through the script as quickly as they can, without hesitation or pauses. You may get to that stage as you drill your presentation or pitch, but the following adaptation is worth trying even if you never become word-perfect.

For each slide or section of the presentation complete the following two phrases out loud:

1. For this section/slide I want the audience to *know*...

2. By the end of the section/slide I want the audience to *feel*...

This technique helps you to focus specifically on the key narrative or takeaways from each moment of the presentation as well as the emotional journey on which you want to take the audience. Run through the presentation again and again as fast as you can speaking the two phrases for each slide or section. If you are presenting as part of a team and more than one person speaks to the slide or the section, you both say the phrases for your messaging. You'll get a feel for the overall flow and a clear sense of how the ideas are ordered and fit together.

● ●

Don't ignore the camera

Drilling virtual or hybrid pitches and presentations requires an additional layer of planning. For maximum cut-through you need to think like a TV or film editor and make some decisions about how you are going to keep your audience engaged. When we're in the room together distractions are normally kept to a minimum but in a virtual environment, the rules seem to be different. I'll deal with how to interact with a virtual audience in the DELIVER phase, so for now we'll look at what to focus on whilst you prepare.

For most people, speaking directly to the camera lens feels very strange. It makes much more logical sense to be looking at the faces of your audience on your screen. Unfortunately, what may, to you, seem like the logical approach, will actually diminish your impact as a speaker. Think about any news broadcast you have ever watched. Where is the reporter looking? The same goes for chat show hosts or daytime TV presenters. When they speak to the audience at home, they look straight down the lens of the camera. You need to get used to doing the same.

It will be impossible to do this all the time of course. You'll want to check in with the faces on your screen. You'll invariably need to glance at your notes, the chat or your slides. But when you're landing a key idea, if you want to come across with maximum gravitas and conviction, you need to deliver it straight to camera.

This requires practice. A low-tech tool to help you get used to this is a sticky note with an arrow on it next to the camera lens. It's a simple and effective reminder to keep you bringing your eye-line back to what feels best for your audience.

If you're using visuals in a virtual presentation this is also something that needs careful choreographic rehearsal. Starting the screen-share at the beginning of the meeting and leaving it up there until you finish is a recipe for disaster. When the sides dominate the virtual screen, we lose human connection. We also unwittingly give our audience permission to disengage, safe in the knowledge that their video feed is now so tiny, that if they start checking their emails or looking at their phone, no one will really be able to see!

Instead, we need plan how we are going to orchestrate the audience's visual experience. Thinking like a film editor, we can change the 'shot' regularly to hold people's interest. Practise sharing the slides and then taking them down to discuss your key ideas. Play with using the 'spotlight' functionality in your virtual meeting software to increase your video size on people's screens. Make sure you bring your hand gestures into frame so that there is visible movement. All these things create a 'pattern interrupt'. The shift in energy and focus plays into the brain's natural tendency to pay attention to movement, especially in your peripheral vision. We're using the same programming that keeps us safe from predators to keep our audience unconsciously reengaging with our message. There's a reason why our favourite shows and influencers put lots of cuts into their edits.

We've already discussed the benefits of filming yourself during rehearsal and when it comes to virtual and hybrid presentations this is a no-brainer. It's so easy to set up a private meeting, hit the record button, deliver your message and then watch it back to see what your audience will be seeing. When you do, you'll instantly spot numerous things you could tweak, not only to improve the narrative but the virtual delivery too.

Whether you're presenting in-person or in front of a camera, another area to prepare for is audience questions.

So that you can see examples of good and bad
virtual presentation technique and slide sharing,
I've created a short video for you to watch at
www.cut-throughbook.com.

 STAND & DELIVER

SET THE STAGE FOR SUCCESS

When rehearsing for virtual and hybrid meetings it's important
to take time to focus on your technical set-up. Getting this right
massively increases your impact on screen. Use the following
checklist before you begin your rehearsals.

✓ Is the camera at eye level so that I can look directly down the
lens?

✓ Am I framed in a medium close-up, with small amount of
space above my head and my shoulders and upper arms
in shot?

✓ Am I using an external microphone if necessary to ensure
good quality sound?

✓ Am I well-lit and using additional lighting if required?

✓ Am I looking directly down the lens to deliver important
messages?

✓ Are my notes and slides close to the camera on screen so
I don't spend lots of time looking away from my audience?

✓ Am I delivering my message at 'level 8' energy? (Standing
will help if you tend to use lower energy.)

✓ Am I using the 'spotlight' functionality to direct the audience's attention?

✓ Am I regularly stopping the screen-share so that I am not hidden behind my slides?

Be aware of these things in every virtual rehearsal and you will quickly develop a more engaging on-screen presence. I also recommend recording at least one of your rehearsals and then reviewing the video against this checklist.

• •

Prepare for Q&A

If you're likely to get questions about your pitch or presentation it is essential that you prepare and rehearse for them. If you're caught off-guard it's easy for your messaging to be derailed and for your carefully crafted narrative to lose its cut-through. There's a five-step process I recommend you use during the 'public rehearsal' phase to get yourself ready.

Step 1: Planning and preparation

The first thing to do is make a list of all the questions you think you might be asked. There will be obvious areas that you'd relish your audience asking about. In fact, you may even construct your presentation in a way that encourages these questions to surface. But equally there will also be questions and topics that you'd rather your audience didn't stray into. The trick is to avoid burying your head in the sand and ignoring these concerns. Instead create a 'worst-case list' of all the things you'd rather not be asked.

Once you've brainstormed all the possible avenues that a Q&A session could take you down, it's time to make sure you have the answers to hand. What additional research or resources do you need at your fingertips in case these things come up? It could be that you need to have notes to hand with the relevant details or even additional slides in an appendix to call on if necessary.

If you're presenting as a team, decide who is going to oversee fielding questions and who will take the lead on questions about different topics. Allocating these responsibilities at this stage will ensure you don't end up talking over each other or coming across as uncertain on the day.

Once the planning and preparation is complete it's time to rehearse how you might answer things in the moment. Invite someone to play the role of the questioner and work through the remaining steps below.

Step 2: State choice and relaxation

One of the key skills to develop when it comes to dealing with audience questions is state choice. By this I mean being able to choose your state of mind and physiological response when under pressure. It's easy when your audience is asking you difficult questions to feel as if you're being interrogated. To feel like people are deliberately trying to trip you up. It may seem deeply personal but often that's just in your head. From time to time, you may experience someone actively trying to catch you out and if that's the case this sequence of steps becomes even more important. But in most cases when you look at your audience's highest intention, they're normally just trying to understand something from their own perspective no matter how obvious it may look from yours.

To help you stay relaxed and in control, as you practise taking questions from the audience, make sure you continue to breathe. We'll look at the power of the breath – as well as a technique for working with it – in the DELIVER phase but as you rehearse the Q&A, work to stay as calm as possible. Often our default response when asked a question is to try to provide our answer as quickly as possible to demonstrate that we know our stuff and are on top of things. Unfortunately, this can make us look desperate or defensive. Instead take your time to hear the question and formulate your answer. Silence is an incredibly powerful tool here. Pausing as you process what you've heard to consider your response increases your gravitas in your audience's eyes.

Step 3: Repeat or paraphrase

Before you can provide an answer, you need to ensure that you have understood what's being asked properly. If there is any doubt in your mind about what the questioner means, it's worth repeating the question or paraphrasing it back. 'What you're asking is...' or 'For clarity, you want to know...'. Taking this approach ensures two things. First, you're able to answer with more precision and, second, you buy yourself some additional time to formulate your answer. I've seen plenty of people tie themselves up in knots and completely derail a presentation by making an assumption about what was being asked and opening a completely unrelated can of worms.

Sometimes it can be worth digging a little deeper at this point too rather than just answering the initial question. If you suspect there is a deeper agenda behind what is being asked, don't shy away from it, lean into it instead. 'So, you're interested in X, Y and Z. Is there anything else that you're concerned about?'. This approach ensures that you get to the heart of any issues rather than skirting around them.

Step 4: Answer succinctly

The first thing to say here is don't bluff! There may be some questions that you don't know the answers to and that's fine. But rather than trying to cover that up, own it. Instead, say something like: 'Thanks for your question. I don't have the answer to hand, but I will take it away and get back to you by X'. This reassures your audience that you are taking their concerns seriously rather than trying to fudge your reply.

When you do have a response to hand, less is definitely more. Don't over answer questions you receive. Especially in a team context, trust that the initial response is good enough unless the audience pushes back or requests further clarification. Over-elaborating with your answer or providing an unsolicited build to a colleague's reply can undermine what's being said. In a group presentation context, it's absolutely acceptable to invite a colleague to build on what you've answered if you think they have particular expertise. But ideally this approach has been agreed in advance and at no point do you cut across each other unrequested.

A useful formula for delivering a pithy response is P + + – P:

P   is your position or proposal

+   is a key reason or piece of evidence that supports your proposal

+   is a second key reason or piece of evidence that supports your proposal

–   is a counter argument and an acknowledgement that other people think differently or support a different approach

P   is your position or proposal restated

This formula is an assertive way of responding when there are differing opinions in the audience as it acknowledges that these exist whilst reinforcing your belief in the approach you are proposing.

Ultimately success during a Q&A comes from creating a shared understanding, so for this reason, don't move on until you're comfortable that your audience is comfortable.

Step 5: Get back on message

Once everyone is happy, your final job is to get things back on track. Rather than putting the ball back in the audience's court where a follow-up question may possibly materialize, if you feel that a satisfactory answer has been provided, move the conversation on. Look for a way to bring things back to one of your key messages so that the interaction finishes on your terms. This plays into the 'peak end rule' that we spoke about earlier. We need to be deliberate about the final thing our audience hears rather than leaving it up to chance.

Use the five steps above to practise for all eventualities. Whilst questions often come at set points in a presentation, it's also worth asking one of your invited audience members in a 'public rehearsal' to interrupt you at random. Learning how to deal with this in the safe space of rehearsals means you're less likely to be caught off guard during the real thing.

Ultimately, we hope for the best and plan for the worst.

 STAND & DELIVER

DRAFT A WORST-CASE LIST

To prepare for the sorts of questions you may get asked, make a 'worst-case list':

- What are the questions that you would find most difficult to answer?
- What are the topics that are most likely to drag the conversation off track?
- Which areas are you least confident talking about?

Brainstorm your own list and then ask people you trust to add to it. Make it as wide ranging and comprehensive as possible.

The very act of creating this list will start to prime your brain to be able to answer the questions. It's also worth allocating some dedicated rehearsal time to work through your responses. Ideally do this with audience members throwing the questions at you during the presentation. Give them permission to ask follow-up questions too if they don't feel satisfied with your answers.

It's better to step out of your comfort zone to practice facing a deliberately aggressive and forensic audience in a 'public rehearsal', than to be blindsided by one in the actual presentation.

● ●

Have a plan B and C

The final part of the DRILL phase is game planning for the different scenarios you might find yourself in. As much as we like to think that things will play out in a predictable manner, there are often too many variables that are beyond our control. It's therefore imperative you've thought through your plan B. I'd recommend you at least have a plan C too!

The things you should give most consideration to are the two Ts: timings and technology.

Whilst you may have been told you have a certain amount of time for your presentation it's always the quickest thing to change: someone else overruns; an important audience member arrives late; the people you're speaking to need to leave early; etc. These things happen all the time. You need to know what you can cut or extend depending on what's being asked of you. Which sections could go if they absolutely had to? What would you love to add if you suddenly got an extra five minutes? It's worth sketching these variations out in your head or on paper in case you're asked to make some changes on the day.

The other thing you need to plan for is tech failure. What will you do if your laptop dies, or you can't connect to the screen? We'll talk about how to set up on the day in the DELIVER phase but whilst you're rehearsing, it's worth deciding on your contingency plans. Ideally, I would recommend you are able to deliver your message even if you have to abandon the technology altogether. After all, the slides are there to reinforce and support your message, they're not the message itself. If you've followed the steps in this book, you should have an extremely compelling narrative to share even if all the equipment you'd planned to use stopped working.

Time and tech often require major adjustments but there are also likely to be numerous micro adjustments you need to make on the day too. These are worth giving some thought to ahead of time as well. In my book, *IMPACT*, I call this 'packing your parachute'. What are the things that would save you in case of emergency? It might be as simple as ensuring you've got a glass of water nearby so that you can buy some thinking time as you sip, or to relieve yourself of a dry mouth. It might be thinking of some questions you could ask your audience if you forget what's coming next. Whatever niggling worries you have about the presentation, make sure you choose an appropriate parachute to use if needed. Don't be afraid to deploy them during the rehearsal period either. Rather than letting rehearsals grind to a halt when things go wrong, get used to testing out your parachute to see if you can use it to smoothly continue the presentation.

Like most things in life the more you practise, the easier it becomes. Time invested in planning and rehearsal is never time wasted.

 STAND & DELIVER

• •

PACK A PARACHUTE

When things go wrong, and at some point in time, they inevitably will, you want to be able to trust that you'll be able to respond effectively. Before you step in front of your actual audience put some safety nets in place.

What will you always have with you? A water bottle? Bullet points on note cards? A spare laptop charger? A bag of connectors? What questions could you ask the audience if you forgot what you were about to say? Who in the audience will you engage with first if no one asks anything?

There are no right or wrong answer here but start to create a list of things that would give you solace.

As you go through the different rehearsal phases build up your list of different parachutes so that you can walk into the room or join the virtual meeting safe in the knowledge that if things go wrong, you have a plan.

• •

Chapter summary

The fourth step of this playbook has been focused on rehearsal and preparation. Your commitment to this process will be the difference between a great presentation and a mediocre one. Great performances may happen in public in front of a live audience, but they're built in private away from prying eyes. This phase is all about experimentation. Failure and mistakes are actively encouraged so that you can start to discover what really works. Whether you're presenting solo or as part of a team you need to build a muscle memory you can rely on when the stakes are high. There are five stages of rehearsal I suggest you work through:

1. The car crash

2. Private rehearsal

3. Public rehearsal

4. Technical rehearsal

5. Dress rehearsal

Make sure you adapt your preparation to the medium in which you are presenting. You'll need to approach in-person differently to virtual, especially if you're presenting as part of a team. For those team presentations a key area of focus should be the transitions between speakers so that the narrative feels smooth and connected.

You also need to plan for the unexpected. Schedule time for the following too:

- ✓ Preparing for Q&A, especially unwanted questions
- ✓ Preparing for changes in timings
- ✓ Preparing for technical difficulties

You can't cover every possible scenario but if you've given some thought to the most likely and the most unwanted, you'll be much better prepared should things veer off track.

Once rehearsals are complete it's time to step out in front of your audience.

Chapter five

DELIVER: Leave them wanting more

Discover > Distil > Design > Drill > **Deliver** > Debrief

Step 5: Deliver

You can have an expertly crafted message, your visuals can be stunning, the structure can be compelling, the stories entertaining and everything can have been rehearsed diligently but ultimately what you'll be remembered for (or not!) is your performance on the day. Of course, everything you have done up to this point will play a part in how successful you are when it comes to speaking up in front of your audience. That's a given. But there are certain things you need to do to capitalize on all your hard work and ensure you cut through.

Step 5 of the playbook is DELIVER and in it I'm going to focus on everything you can do on the day of the presentation to maximize your success. This stage of the process is where the rubber meets the road. Where you share with your audience the fruits of all the hard work that has gone on behind the scenes.

Just like the earlier steps in this playbook, this phase is not something that should be left to chance. The more systematic you are in your approach the more comfortable and in command you will feel. Whether you're an introvert or an extrovert, a seasoned presenter or a first-time speaker, you need to be able to engage authentically with your audience so that they listen to your message.

It's time to explore how to show up at your best, but first let's deal with the elephant in the room.

Ditch the nerves

I don't know a single person who hasn't experienced the symptoms of nerves when speaking in front of an audience at some point in their life. Even if the feelings were fleeting, all the top speakers I have worked with, interviewed and spoken to, describe a change in state before they first open their mouths. When I first arrived at drama school, I was an incredibly nervous performer. I loved the buzz I got from being on stage, but I would get very anxious before the curtain went up. Now, when I speak in front of an audience those symptoms are greatly reduced, but, for me, they never fully go away. What has changed significantly however, is my attitude towards them.

What I've come to realize, is that nerves are just energy. In fact, the symptoms of nerves and the symptoms of excitement are indistinguishable. Imagine you visited your doctor and described what you experienced when speaking in public: increased heart rate, sweating more, being focused on future events. Without you giving it a label, your doctor would struggle to differentiate between a diagnosis of fear or exhilaration. I'm not necessarily suggesting that you try to trick yourself into believing that presenting is exciting if that's not how you feel about it. But I do think it's worth exploring how you can use the energy of the situation, rather than allowing it to use you. Even if you really enjoy being in front of an audience, you need to ensure that you're in the driving seat and your emotions aren't calling the shots.

When it comes to shifting your mindset there are a couple of important things to bear in mind. The first is that your audience wants you to succeed. For the most part when we see someone struggling when they present, we have massive empathy for them. No one in their right mind walks into a meeting, joins a virtual call or sits down to listen to someone speak and thinks to themselves 'I really hope this is a complete waste of my time'! People want what you have to say to be interesting and relevant. We need to get out of the habit of thinking that people want to trip us up. They might want to ensure what we say is accurate, they may even have a different opinion but it's highly unlikely that the people listening to you are actively willing you to fail.

No matter how important the pitch or presentation it's also worth taking control and lowering the stakes for ourselves. It's very unlikely to be life or death. If you miss a few sentences or gabble your words, will anyone really care? In fact, when things go wrong your audience only normally notices if you point it out or apologize. Unless you're a politician publishing your script to the press, no one knows what is or isn't about to come out of your mouth. Often the best approach is to keep calm and carry on.

One technique I find incredibly useful to positively shift your focus, is setting yourself some 'quick wins'. Too often we delay gratification, we decide we'll only be happy or feel successful once the whole thing is over and we have achieved our goal. Instead, a useful strategy is to set yourself a series of 'quick wins'; micro goals that are relatively easy to achieve. It could be a simple as walking into the room and making positive eye contact as you shake the hands of the people around the table. It could be getting up the steps onto stage without falling over. Or successfully delivering the *S.T.A.R.* opening you've planned and rehearsed. When we set ourselves these early goals and then go on to accomplish them, we get a healthy hit of dopamine which makes us feels good and spurs us on.

So rather than worrying what people are thinking about you, take the spotlight off yourself and shine it on your audience. If you really focus on their needs and getting your message across to them in the way that resonates, you won't have time to worry what they think about you. Instead, you'll be too busy serving them, which is what all the best speakers do. There is, however, one thing that is vital to do before you kick things off.

Stop before you start

Whenever the stakes are high, adrenaline kicks in and works like an accelerator. Before we know it, we've rushed straight into our presentation without taking the slightest pause. Unfortunately, that speed can often undermine us. We come across as hurried or nervous. Instead, we need to stop before we start. The most compelling speakers appear to be in control, they take their time, they seem to own the stage or their seat around the meeting room table. We need to break the unconscious instinct to jump straight in and start speaking. The way to do this is to take a deep breath.

In the Sunday Times bestseller, *Breath*, author James Nestor unpicks the science behind a process we repeat unconsciously 25,000 times a day. It turns out that if we want to relax, we need to slow things down. 'Breathing is an autonomic function we can consciously control. While we can't simply decide when to slow or speed up our heart or digestion, or move blood from one organ to another, we can choose how and when to breathe. Willing ourselves to breathe slowly will open up the communication along the vagal network and relax us into a parasympathetic state.'[1]

While I was training to be an actor we did a lot of breath work. It was a way to fuel the voice but also a powerful tool for centring and reducing stage fright. What I began to notice was that whenever I felt nervous, my breathing became more shallow and much quicker. Shorter breaths high up in the chest rather than longer breaths from the diaphragm. It's this low diaphragmatic breath that we want to harness. It reduces our cortisol and increases our testosterone, leaving us less stressed and more confident. The popularity of mindfulness and yoga have brought awareness to the power that working with the breath can have and it's a toolkit we can use whenever we pitch and present.

If you find you've got off to a speedy start you can definitely use slow diaphragmatic breathing to help relax you, but my recommendation is to work with these tools before you walk into the room or join the virtual meeting. This means you begin from a place of relaxation and calm and are much less likely to get triggered in the first place. I'll share two specific techniques you can use in the next 'stand and deliver' section. Whichever you choose, include it in your preparation.

Whenever I'm presenting at a conference, for the ten minutes before I speak, I'm focused on my breath. I don't need to be mediating in a dark room, I can be sitting next to the CEO and listening to the other presenters but in the background, I'm preparing myself to begin from a place of calm. When it's my turn to speak I also make a point of pausing for one final breath before I open my mouth. This allows me to ensure I'm speaking from a place of clarity – by bringing oxygen to the prefrontal cortex of my brain – and gives me a second to connect with my audience and collect my thoughts before I launch in.

To supercharge the power of the breath it's also worth paying attention to what you're doing with your body.

STAND & DELIVER

• •

TAKE A DEEP BREATH

Focusing on your breath before you start presenting will help you begin with confidence, which in turn will give your audience confidence in what you have to say. In an ideal world practice the diaphragmatic breathing technique I'm about to share well in advance of your presentation and then repeat it in the five to ten minutes before you speak. If you need to change your state quickly, a few rounds of box breathing should do the trick.

Diaphragmatic breathing

Get both feet on the ground and relax your body as much as possible. Scan from the top of your head all the way to your toes and if you notice any tension allow it to release. Pay particular attention to your abdominal muscles. These should be relaxed, allowing your belly to expand as you breathe in. If it helps, place a hand just below your belly button and observe the natural expansion and contraction as you breathe deeply. Keep doing this for a couple of minutes. With an increase in relaxation and focus your breath will start to slow. Notice your breathing pattern in this calm and confident state. How many seconds do you breathe in for? How many seconds do you breathe out for? There's no right or wrong answer here. Just pay attention to what you do naturally. This is your personal formula for relaxed diaphragmatic breathing. Concentrate on replicating this pattern in the build-up to any important presentation so that you start from a place of relaxation.

Box breathing

This is a technique used by U.S. Navy SEALs to stay calm and focused. Use it as a quick and powerful reset mechanism if you start to experience the symptoms of stress or nerves. As above it will work best if you can relax your body as much as possible and get yourself grounded by placing both feet on the floor. Inhale for a count of four. Hold for a count of four. Exhale for a count of four. Hold for a count of four. Repeat for at least six rounds. It may help to imagine you are drawing one side of a box with each stage of the breath.

 For video and audio guides to both these breathing techniques visit www.cut-throughbook.com.

Warm up your instrument

Athletes warm up. Musicians warm up. Actors warm up. It would seem crazy to most high performers to step onto their chosen field of play without doing something in advance to get themselves 'in the zone'. And yet, working with people in business for over a decade, I've discovered that very few have a replicable set of steps to ensure they perform at their best. If you want to maximize your impact and influence, I'd suggest you make time to warm up before you perform. There are two area to focus on. Your physical warm-up and your vocal warm-up. In the Presence chapter of my book, *IMPACT*, I talk in detail about the importance of your physical and vocal performance but from a pitch and presentation perspective there are a few simple things to bear in mind.

First, from a body language point of view we need to ensure we are open and expansive. This is true whether we're engaging in-person or virtually. When we get stressed or nervous these things show up as tension in the body. We'll notice a contraction in the muscles and often we'll close ourselves physically to protect ourselves. This can manifest as slumped shoulders, crossed arms or just slight tension especially, in the shoulders, neck and face. These changes may be a matter of millimetres but their negative impact on our audience can be huge, so we need to work to combat them.

Before you present, make time to move. I'll share a few of my favourite warm-up ideas in the next 'stand and deliver' section but do whatever works best for you. Take a few moments to identify where you are holding tension and then do what you need to do to release it. It could be shoulder rolls, it could be star jumps or a much more subtle body scan. The key is to ensure that you do what's necessary to begin from a place of physical relaxation and expansion. It's not about dominating the space, which can come across as aggressive. Instead, it's about holding your own ground and being physically present.

Pay attention to your energy as you warm up too. We talked in the DRILL phrase about the concept of 'level 8'. It's important as part of your preparation to reconnect with this. What do you need to do to ensure you have instant access to this performance state? If you tend to default to a lower energy level, this preparation is especially important. If you tend to default to a level 9 or 10, how do you contain things, so you don't overwhelm your audience?

The second part of your warm-up should be vocal. After all, it's your voice that will carry your ideas to your audience's ears. Especially if your presentation will be the first significant words you have spoken to another human being that day, preparing your voice for performance is essential. Actors and singers will often spend significant time warming up their voices before a show but even a few minutes will help you produce a more engaging sound. There are two vocal elements to prioritize: resonance and clarity.

When the voice lacks resonance, the emotion behind your message fails to carry. This is usually the result of vocal tightness. Think of the voice as a muscle. In order to free it up we want to gently stretch things without causing strain. The easiest way to do this is to hum. Choose your favourite song and hum it. It doesn't even need to be loud. This simple act is enough to start to free up vocal tension and help you access a greater pitch range, making your voice more free and expressive.

Once you've worked on your resonance for a minute or two, it's time to work on your articulation. This is about engaging the 43 muscles in the face to help you get your mouth around the words. Whether it's lip trills, face stretches or tongue twisters you'll want to do something that gets the mask of the face moving. This is especially important for virtual presentations as your face is pretty much all your audience is going to see on screen. The more warmed up and expressive it is, the more committed to your message you will seem. The great thing about warming up the muscles of articulation is that they automatically improve your clarity too. You're literally better able to articulate your message. If you tend to speak quickly, have a strong accent or are presenting in a second language this part of the warm-up is especially important.

Whatever warm-up you decide on, timing is key. The closer it is to when you perform the more effective and impactful it is going to be. However, you obviously can't start doing tongue twisters or lunges in the middle of a meeting, so you need to plan things accordingly. Even if you're forced to do your warm-up a few hours before you actually speak, it will be better than nothing. Your job then becomes to maintain that relaxed and open energy whilst you wait, so you avoid letting tension creep in. As with most things, the more your practise, the easier it becomes.

Once you're ready to perform there are a few other things to pay attention to.

 STAND & DELIVER

• •

PLAN YOUR WARM-UP

It's worth planning a series of warm-up routines in advance so you don't have to think about it on the big day. I'd suggest a 90-second version for when time is limited, a five-minute version you can do immediately before you present, and a fuller 10–20-minute version if there's going to be a significant gap between your warm-up and your performance. Split them into physical and vocal exercises. The following are my go-to techniques, but your warm-up should be your own, so do what works for you. For your physical warm-up, these can be the same sort of movements you do before you play sport or go for a run. Whatever helps you elevate your energy whilst staying relaxed.

Physical warm-up

Shoulder and neck mobilization

This is an area where we tend to hold a lot of tension. Gently roll the shoulders backwards five to ten times. Next, squeeze them up towards your ears and sigh out as you allow them to drop repeating five to ten times. Finally, give your neck and shoulders a massage to release any remaining tension.

Full body energization

One limb at a time, shake out your hands, arms, feet and legs. This is a good way to get the blood pumping.

Full body twists for flexibility

Start with your feet shoulder-width apart and your arms hanging by your sides. Twist your body from the waist so that you're looking behind yourself. Alternate from one side to the other letting the weight of your arms generate momentum. The movement should be free and relaxed.

Vocal warm-up

Humming for resonance

Choose a familiar tune and hum it gently on a 'mmmm' sound.

Pitch glides

Staying with a 'mmmm' sound, allow your voice to glide from the lowest note you can make, to the highest note you can make. Continue to siren up and down. This allows you to explore your full range.

Face stretches

To engage the muscles of articulation, alternate between stretching your whole face into a massive silent scream and then screwing everything tightly towards your nose. Repeat three to six times.

Tongue precision

The placement of your tongue in your mouth dictates the sounds you create. Warm up your tongue by alternating between a pointed tongue and a wide flat tongue.

Tongue twisters

Bring everything together by reciting a few of your favourite tongue twisters. This allows you to work on resonance and clarity. Increase the speed to increase the challenge.

 For videos of these exercises and some of the other physical and vocal warmups I use before an important pitch or presentation visit www.cut-throughbook.com.

Check the tech

Few things are as stressful when you're presenting as when tech fails. Whether it's difficulty connecting to the screen, problems dialling into the meeting or a clicker that won't click, we need to minimize the chance of trouble. Don't leave things up to chance. Anything you can do to mitigate problems in advance will mean you can focus on the important stuff when the time to present comes.

In an ideal world I would suggest conducting some sort of final tech check at least ten minutes before you start. If you can get access to the venue the night before, or even a few hours in advance, so much the better. You don't want your audience's first impression to be of you bent over a table fiddling with some leads! Hopefully you've done the 'technical rehearsal' suggested in the DRILL phase, so you're familiar with how everything works. On the day it should just be a case of plugging everything in and giving it a final test.

For virtual presentations getting online ten minutes before your audience joins is non-negotiable. With software updates and compatibility issues the chances of something not working are significantly heightened. You need to check that cameras and mics are connected, you have permission to share your screen, and you can see any chat or polling features you may be planning to use. Don't be put off by an organizer's or an administrator's laid-back approach to this. If something goes wrong it will be you with egg on your face not them, so insist politely that they accommodate your request.

Whether you're delivering in-person or online, it's also worth having a back-up plan just in case. I can't count the number of times I have asked the venue in advance what connectors their projectors or screens use only to turn up and find I need something different. I always carry my own bag of leads, connectors and spares. Everything I need to make the tech work. I often even have a version of the slides on my phone and an adaptor that would allow me to run my presentation from it in case of emergency.

Taking ten minutes in advance to ensure that everything is working properly, and the room is set up as you want it allows you to relax and focus on what you're going to say. After all, as we've already established getting the opening right is vital.

Start with a bang

When I shared how to craft your *S.T.A.R.* opening in the DESIGN phase I mentioned the importance of first impressions. Thus far we've been mainly focused on the words, but we mustn't overlook the power of your physical presence to create cut-through either. How you walk into the room, step onto the stage or first appear on camera matters. If you're fidgety and can't make eye contact, you'll instantly lose people's trust. If you're too domineering people will switch off or zone out. It's essential to get the balance right. In the Presence chapter of my book, *IMPACT*, I share in detail, how to work on your posture and body language to increase your gravitas. The most important thing is to take up space.

If you've warmed up properly, focusing on being open and expansive, your job is to hold on to those physical sensations and not allow yourself to become small under pressure. If you're shaking hands with your audience, maintain eye contact and stay relaxed. If you're presenting from stage, find a moment to stand still and look out at the crowd. If you're on camera, smile and look down the lens. All these actions signal to your audience that you are neither a threat, nor are you threatened. You reassure them that they're in safe hands.

Of course, not all audiences are ready to listen. If we're pumped up and ready to go but they're disinterested and tired, we may come across as over the top. The important thing about the start of your presentation from an energy perspective is to meet your audience where they are and take them to where you want them to be. If we go back to our 1 to 10 energy scale, we've already established that what you're aiming for is 'level 8'. However, if when you walk into the room your audience is at a 3, your 'level 8' energy could feel like a slap round the face! You never need your audience to be at the same level as you. In fact, that would be problematic as you might end up competing with them for the spotlight. But we don't want the difference between them and us to be too great. When faced with a low-energy audience your job is to go in just a few points above them and slowly warm up the room.

Those first moments of connection, before you begin the presentation proper, are all about building rapport. You want your audience to feel loved. They need your undivided attention and focus. They need to feel you want to be there. Even in the most formal pitch settings you still need to work to engage your audience from the offset. The more things feel like a relaxed conversation rather than a rigid monologue, the more likely you are to convince people of what you have to say. Resist the urge to worry about what's coming next and instead stay present in the moment so that you kick things off in the right way.

If you're pitching or presenting virtually there are a few additional things I recommend that you consider.

Don't forget to unmute

Virtual or hybrid pitches and presentations aren't better or worse. They're just different. All the foundational techniques we've talked about so far apply but when it comes to the final performance there are a few important things you need to think about. We discussed how to prepare and rehearse for this type of meeting in the DRILL phase. Now we need to ensure that you maximize your cut-through from the word go.

My first blindingly obvious piece of advice is don't forget to unmute. I'm only being slightly flippant here. I still regularly join meetings where people are happily chatting away with their microphones switched off. It all comes back to the wider issue of being familiar with the tech. You don't want to be upstaged, so make sure you know your audience can hear you before you speak, to bolster that first impression. I also recommend that you mute your microphone when you're not speaking to limit the chance of background noise pulling focus.

Another vital piece of housekeeping when presenting virtually is checking your camera framing before you join. All major meeting software gives you a preview window before you click to enter the meeting room. Use this to check how you are being seen by your audience. You should be in what's known in the film world as a medium closeup. There should be a small gap between your head and the top of the frame (not a massive empty void!) and your shoulders and upper arms should be in shot. This mean the audience's view of you is the same as if they were sitting across the boardroom table from you. It also means that when you gesticulate your hands will naturally come into shot too. The camera should be at eye level so that you meet your audience head on, rather than looking up or down at them. These things are small, but they make a massive difference to how you are perceived.

Whilst you were rehearsing you should have been practising getting used to looking directly down the lens of the camera. My suggestion when it comes to delivering the presentation live is to be aware of this but not to obsess about it. We know that first impressions are vital, so be sure to look at the camera as you join and as you greet people. Delivering your *S.T.A.R.* opening direct to camera is incredibly powerful too and will increase the impact of your message. Once that's done you can be more fluid. Try to come back to the lens when you can, especially for key messages and for answering questions. Most importantly, avoid being distracted by anything on a second screen or on your desk. You don't want you audience thinking you are checking your emails rather than engaging with them!

Another thing to be aware of when presenting virtually is your energy. 'Level 8' is an essential here. The problem is the camera sucks energy from your performance. I learned this very early on in my acting career. It's not about jazz hands. It's about focus. If you've ever watched a recording of yourself speaking, you may have noticed you come across as a bit flat. It's a trick of the camera but it's worth paying attention to. When presenting virtually you need to turn things up. You need to take responsibility for the energy of the situation and do what you can to lift it. If you've done your warm-up this should be easy. For most people it's worth aiming for a 'Level 8.5' on camera, just slightly more energized than you would be face-to-face to compensate for the digital distortion.

Once you've got your own performance sorted it's time to focus on your audience. Unless you're delivering a keynote or TEDx style presentation, bringing your audience into the conversation early on is vital. To be honest even if you're being asked to deliver something more 'broadcast' style, it's still worth bearing these things in mind. I like to imagine virtual pitches and presentations like a dinner party. As the presenter you are the host. It's your job to make everyone feel welcome and relaxed. If people were coming to your house for dinner, you'd greet them at the front door. You'd ask them how they were. You'd show them into the room where everyone was gathered or take them to their seat. You'd introduce them to other people they didn't know. You'd give them an indication of when the food was being served and what was on the menu. I could go on but hopefully the parallels are clear. The more you can take charge, the easier your audience will find it to relax and listen.

A few words on hybrid presentations here too. Dealing with an on-screen audience and an in-person audience simultaneously is tricky. It's even harder if you're dialling in and the majority of those you are speaking to are in a room together. In these hybrid scenarios you need to be even more assertive. Use people's names. Lay out your expectation for how you want to run things up front and get their buy in. Avoid long monologues, and look for frequent opportunities to connect. If you're in the room and some of your audience are dialling in, make sure you engage with those on camera early. When it comes to Q&A make sure you deliberately check back in with them too. People joining virtually are much less likely to interrupt or ask questions, so you need to encourage them to participate.

For solo presentations you're going to have to do everything yourself (unless you invite someone to join you as tech support which I highly recommend). For virtual team presentations I suggest you divide and conquer. Assign team members specific roles to free up the person speaking to concentrate on delivering the message. Decide on who's managing the waiting room, who's controlling the slides, who's watching the chat. I'd also suggest assigning someone to monitor the audience's reactions. When you're presenting it's hard to pay attention to all the tiny faces on your screen and harder still to discern how your message is landing with them. Make it someone's job to keep an eye on the audience's video feeds and notice what's going on. Are people looking disengaged or confused? Does someone have a question? Decide in advance how you will bring these observations to the attention of the person speaking to ensure maximum audience engagement.

Virtual and hybrid presentations can be just as impactful as in-person ones as long as you acknowledge the differences and adapt accordingly. But whatever the format, one of the keys to success is audience engagement. Let's look at how to optimize it.

 To watch a short video on my top tip for lighting, camera and sound for virtual and hybrid presentations visit www.cut-throughbook.com.

 STAND & DELIVER

USE A CHECKLIST

When the stakes are high it's easy to forget things which is why I highly recommend you create a 'pre-presentation checklist' to ensure that you get off to the right start. By the time they get their licence, pilots have many hours of flying under their belts. But even though they know what to do inside out and back to front they're not allowed to start to taxi until they have completed their pre-flight checks. The simple act of ticking things off ensures that nothing can get missed out in the heat of the moment.

I have a different checklist for in-person presentations and virtual ones as the requirements are different. These lists are a mixture of technical checks I want to make and warm-up routines and rituals that I like to complete before I start. I would encourage you to create your own. What do you need to do in the days, hours and minutes before you present to put your mind at rest? Which warm-up routines or rituals get you in the zone?

• •

• •

 To download my 'pre-presentation checklists' to use as a template, or to cross-check your own against, visit www.cut-throughbook.com.

• •

Stop the tumbleweed

Whilst it's not always appropriate to get your audience participating in your pitch or presentation, engagement is non-negotiable. They don't have to speaking aloud, but even in a more broadcast-style keynote speech, your audience needs to be part of the metaphorical conversation. If they're not, you're talking *at* them rather than *with* them and I guarantee they will very quickly lose interest and switch off. In fact, the best speakers make us feel like they're talking directly to us, however many people are in the room.

We'll look first at some techniques for creating connection with bigger audiences where a full dialogue isn't viable and then I'll share some thoughts on how to avoid the tumbleweed and awkward silence if you do want the pitch or presentation to be more conversational. Even in more formal settings, look for opportunities to blend the two approaches. I don't know anyone (except for a comedian friend) who's come off stage or walked out of a meeting and said, 'I really wish I'd had less engagement'!

One of the quickest and easiest ways to draw people in is to use rhetorical questions. This is a brilliant technique because if you ask someone a question, the human brain finds it very difficult not to answer it. How often have you seen someone use this technique? – See. You just did a quick memory scan to look for examples! Ask the question, then give your audience a couple of seconds of silence so that they can ruminate – this is the key to getting them to engage. Then, once they're thinking, continue with your presentation.

Another similar technique you'll see used by a lot of professional speakers, is to ask the audience to raise a hand. 'By a show of hands, who here has experienced X'. Again, this is a great way to drive active participation. You need to ask with conviction but as soon as one person raises their arm, others will feel safe to follow. If you're going to use this approach, I'd actually recommend that you raise a hand as you ask the question too. The visual cue is very powerful, and your audience is much more likely to respond. Doing it this way also means you can be more subtle in your request. Raising an arm as you say, 'Who here has experienced X?' should be enough to get your audience onboard.

My final tip for large audiences is to tap into their imaginations. Obviously, this works equally well for more intimate settings too. We've already discussed the power of storytelling in the DESIGN phase and any story you share will draw your audience into your subject matter. But even starting a sentence with the word 'Imagine…' makes it impossible for your audience to resist joining the dots for themselves. Once they can picture what you're talking about in their minds-eye, they're with you. And if what you're asking them to imagine is the outcome you are looking to achieve, you're already halfway to achieving it!

For situations where you're looking for deeper engagement you have more tools at your disposal. The most powerful of these is setting the frame of the conversation. Think about this like agreeing the rules of the game before you start playing. In order to have an enjoyable experience everyone needs to be on the same page. Whether you are presenting virtually or in-person, your audience needs to know what to expect and you need to get their agreement to the approach you are suggesting. In *IMPACT* I share seven different frames you can use in a variety of settings but in a presentation or pitch context the 'structure frame' and the 'open frame' are the most useful.

An 'open frame' is about encouraging continuous dialogue. Do you want questions throughout? If so, be explicit with your audience that this is what you're looking for. They might not be initially forthcoming, so if you want to nurture this sort of conversation you have to stop regularly and ask for questions or comments.

If you'd prefer them to wait for a designated Q&A section, I'd suggest you set a structure frame. Tell them where during the presentation you're going to be taking questions and then honour that commitment.

The trick to using both frames is to lay out the ground rules and then use the magic words 'is that ok?'. If you get nods, or 'yeses' a contract has been formed between you and your audience, and you can remind them of it later to improve participation.

When asking people for questions, another thing to remember is not to put them on the spot. If you've been talking for ten minutes straight and then out of nowhere ask 'Any questions?' you're likely to see a sea of slightly startled faces. At that point, it's unlikely anyone will have anything on the tip of their tongue. Instead, get good at signposting and seeding when opportunities for audience participation are coming up. Saying something like 'I've got a final slide I'd like to cover and then I'd love to hear your questions' lets the audience know that they need to get their thinking caps on.

Consider the language you use too. Rather than using the standard 'Any questions?', when you're ready for their engagement switch your request to 'What questions do you have?'. This has a linguistic presupposition that there are questions in the room. If you're brave enough to use the phrase and then, importantly, to pause, I will guarantee that someone will engage. All too often we don't give our audience enough time to think. The more you embrace silence and allow them to process, the more fruitful the interactions will become. In reality, what seems like a massive pause for us, is much shorter from the audience's perspective. It takes confidence but the results are transformational.

My final tip for maximizing engagement and avoiding tumbleweed is to use people's names. When we hear our name being used, we instantly feel like part of the conversation. Phrases like 'I know this is a topic close to Sara's heart' or 'I'm sure Paulo will have questions about this' show that you are connected to your audience. For the people that you name-check this is even more pronounced. If you notice certain voices aren't being heard and you would like to draw them in, it's also worth being direct. 'Alisha, do you have any questions or thoughts on this?' is a gentle way to provide space for someone to re-engage with the topic. This is especially important in a pitch context where there will be key decision makers and influencers that you'll want to be part of the conversation.

Whilst engagement is usually a good thing, there may be instances where questions or comments could be derailing so let's look next at how you deal with those sorts of scenarios.

Handle any objections

You've prepped for Q&A in the DRILL phase but sometimes you move beyond the need to politely and concisely answer questions into what often feels more like objection handling. This doesn't just happen in a sales or pitching context either. Sometimes someone in your audience will take exception to something you've said, or you'll get a feeling that there is opposition to the idea you are sharing. Don't resist this or shy away from it. Rather than something to fear, this is a golden opportunity. It's much better to surface any negativity during the presentation, rather than let the audience leave only to find out later that they weren't fully onboard.

Your objective should be to transform any objections into moments that actually strengthen your pitch. To do this effectively here are five steps you need to follow.

1. Reveal

You need to make sure you acknowledge the elephant in the room. Rather than skirting around opposing views or opinions, call them out. Ask people what resistance they have to the ideas you are sharing. Do whatever you can to reveal any hidden objections. Once they're out in the open you can engage with them. If they remain invisible, you're flying blind. A great question to ask in a pitch context is 'what would stop you saying yes?'. If you feel like there's something unspoken, your job is to draw it out. The best way to do this is to say what you see. Articulate any reactions you notice or feelings you have about how your message is being received. 'I notice' or 'I feel' are good ways to open the conversation. 'I notice you look concerned' or 'I feel there might be differing opinions in the room'.

2. Relate

Once things are out in the open you need to engage with them. You don't want to close the conversation down. You need to show that you're ready to listen not just to speak. This is all about putting money into the emotional bank account and building trust with your audience. Use phrases like 'That's interesting. Can you walk me through your concerns', 'I had a feeling you might say that', 'I can see why you might think that' and 'Can you tell me more?'. These buy you time to respond fully and show that you're interested in hearing other perspectives.

3. Refine

It may feel counterintuitive but at this point rather than trying to overcome the objection I'd encourage you to go deeper. In most instances you don't have enough information to respond effectively. What's being shared by your audience at this point is normally just the surface layer. By going deeper – a simple question like 'is there anything else?' usually works well here – you gain greater understanding of their perspective. This second round of questioning will normally get you to the detail layer, but you'll need to ask again if you want to get to the core. This is all about listening to understand, rather than listening to respond. Three layers deep – surface, detail, core – is a great rule of thumb to help you get to the heart of your audience's concern. Once you've uncovered the objection fully, play it back to them in your own words to demonstrate that you grasp their point of view.

4. Reduce

Now that you know what you're really dealing with you can start to transform it. Einstein is supposed to have said something along the lines of 'a problem cannot be solved at the same level it was created' – it's sound advice. If you want to reduce the size of the objection for your audience, you need them to see the problem from a different perspective. Normally that means getting them out of the weeds and back up to the big picture. Focus on where you already have agreement and demonstrate that you have more in common than in conflict. 'Yes and' is a useful phrase here. Often people see their objections as binary. If you can show them that both ways of seeing things can co-exist, their objection suddenly has less potency.

5. Redirect

Your final task is to redirect the conversation. You don't want to get stuck in the objection space forever. Once you are satisfied that you have shifted their perspective sufficiently (or resolved that they are immovable) it's time to take back control of the presentation and move things on. This is especially important if it seems to be a single audience member who has a concern. Often everyone else is sitting there willing this detour from the main topic to be over. If you need to, offer to have a one-to-one conversation in due course or suggest that you get back to them with more information at a later date. It's important to reconnect with your *know, feel, do, now* for the presentation at this stage, giving particular focus to the emotional journey you want to take your audience on. If you're wildly off track, it's time to course correct.

Taking these five steps will help you handle objections elegantly without coming across as defensive or dismissive. Embrace the opportunity to engage with your audience openly and it will enhance your credibility and demonstrate your belief in your message.

Chapter summary

The fifth step of this playbook is about performing at your best on the big day. The more prepared you are, the more flexible you can be. To be a top performer in any field you need to put in the work and pitches and presentations are no different. This phase is about building the muscles of performance. Knowing what you need to do to get yourself in the zone and how to set yourself up for success. We want to control the controllables and then remain adaptable so that we can navigate any obstacles with ease.

To supercharge your delivery focus on the following:

✓ Reframing your nerves and understanding that your audience want you to succeed

✓ Mastering your breath and learning to stop before you start

✓ Developing a warm-up that gets you ready to perform

✓ Creating a checklist to control the tech

✓ Opening with the right energy to draw your audience in

✓ Tweaking your virtual delivery to make it more impactful

✓ Connecting with your audience to drive engagement

✓ Using the five Rs – reveal, relate, refine, reduce, redirect – to handle any objections

The tools I've outlined will allow you to deliver your message with more confidence and credibility, ensuring that the carefully crafted ideas you are sharing cut though.

It's important to realize however, that the process doesn't finish the moment you leave the room or end the virtual meeting.

Chapter six

DEBRIEF: Enjoy the accolades and learn from the critics

Discover >> Distil >> Design >> Drill >> Deliver >> **Debrief**

Step 6: Debrief

For any athlete at the top of their game, the post-performance review is a key part of their development process. Doing the video analysis is non-negotiable. It's how they learn and improve. Unfortunately, the same can't be said in the world of pitches and presentations. Most people are so relieved to get everything over and done with, that the moment it's finished they think that their work is done. However, in many respects it's only just started.

Step 6 of this playbook is DEBRIEF. It's the step that marks the biggest difference between the amateur and the pro. It may be the shortest step but it's arguably the most important. If we don't learn from our performance, we can't expand and grow. Each and every presentation is an opportunity to move towards mastery. Some will go brilliantly. Some will be a disaster. Many will be somewhere in between. Every single one is a chance to get better.

The best speakers on the planet all gave terrible performances early on in their careers. The best creators on YouTube all have early content that sucks. Cut-through isn't something you're born with, it's something you develop. Learning how to evaluate your performance will fast-track your results.

Review your performance

When it comes to debriefing your pitch or presentation don't leave anything up to chance. Life is busy. Diaries are full. If you wait until after you've finished to start thinking about what you can learn, you're already too late. Instead book a 'wash-up session' into your calendar when you are booking in your rehearsals. This session should take place within 24 hours of the presentation itself. Longer than that and memories start to fade and some of the detail might be lost. If you're working as part of a team, it means you need to get everyone in the same room or on the same virtual call.

At this stage we're looking at self-analysis. Capturing your instant reaction to how things went. Of course, you can supplement your findings as you continue to receive formal and informal feedback, but we also want to review your initial impressions. If you're pitching, it's very unlikely you will know the outcome in the first 24 hours but in many respects that's a good thing as it means your analysis won't be blurred by whether you won or lost.

If the presentation was virtual and you were lucky enough to be able to record it, make the debrief a two-step process. Note your first impressions before you watch it back and then continue with the video analysis. The reason for this is to avoid being hyper critical. Your audience experienced your presentation live. Viewing a recording puts things under the microscope. When we watch our own performance back, we tend to focus on all the negatives rather than the many positives that are right in front of our nose. Be mindful of this.

There are many different models from the world of coaching that you can use to evaluate how things went. Each has their strengths and weaknesses. Choose something that is easy to implement and feels proportionate to the situation. If the presentation was five minutes long you don't need to spend three hours raking over every word that you uttered!

Here are three of my favourite review tools.

1. WWWEBI

'What went well? Even better if?'. This is a beautifully simple way to reflect on how things went. Make a list of the things that were successful and a list of the things you could improve. If you spend just five minutes after every presentation answering those two questions, you'll quickly build up a picture of the development areas you need to focus on.

2. What? So what? Now what?

This model was developed Professors Gary Rolfe, Dawn Freshwater and Melanie Jasper.[1] It's another simple framework for engaging in critical thinking.

What?

Describe the presentation – what was delivered and how it went.

So what?

Reflect on the importance – what worked, what didn't, and what was the impact.

Now what?

Plan your next actions – what you'll improve or change next time.

3. SWOT

SWOT analysis is normally thought of a business planning tool, but the framework can also be applied effectively to evaluate a presentation and is especially useful when debriefing pitches.

Strengths

What resonated with the audience? What worked well?

Weaknesses

Which aspects didn't go smoothly? What would you do differently next time?

Opportunities

What are potential areas for follow-up? How could you expand on your ideas next time?

Threats

What were the objections or obstacles? What can you learn from the competition?

Whichever tool you choose to use, the objective is to learn and improve, not to beat yourself up. One of my favourite sayings from the world of Neuro Linguistic Programming is 'there is no failure, only feedback'. If things didn't go as planned use the experience as a way to help you get better in the future.

I'd also recommend that your DEBRIEF phase focuses on the whole process not just the final presentation. Give some thought to what went on at each of the stages.

Discover

How well did you do your research? Is there anything you missed? Did you find out enough about your audience in advance? Did you pick the right team? Did you understand the competition?

Distil

How clearly did you articulate your intention? Did you create an engaging headline? Were your key messages clear? Was there a compelling call to action? Did you find the right stories, examples and case studies to support your argument?

Design

How engaging was the *S.T.A.R.* opening? Did you choose the most appropriate *1.2.3.* middle section? Was your *S.A.L.T.* close powerful and compelling enough? Did the visuals support your message effectively?

Drill

Did you rehearse your presentation enough? If presenting as a team, did you practice your transitions? Were you prepared for any Q&A? Did you have a plan B or plan C? Did you experiment with the tech?

Deliver

How effective was your warm-up? Did you manage your nerves? Were there any tech issues? How well did you create engagement? Were you able to handle any objections?

Obviously, there are myriad other questions you could ask about each playbook phase. These are just a starter. But by reviewing your presentation through this lens you will start to understand where the gaps are in your process and how you can begin to fill them. If you were presenting as part of a team, think about things from the perspective of both your personal performance and your team performance too.

Self-reflection is vital but as I said right at the beginning of this book, none of this about you, it's all about your audience. To really learn and grow, we need to find out how things landed with them.

 To download the list of the DEBRIEF questions above to use as part of your 'wash up session' visit www.cut-throughbook.com.

Ask for feedback

Not all feedback is created equal. Being told you were 'great' or that your presentation was 'really interesting' might feel nice, but it doesn't teach you very much! When we're seeking feedback, the real gold is in the specifics. How you get feedback from your audience will differ depending on the context of your pitch or presentation but what you're asking for is information you can act on rather than generalizations.

First, let's think about how to go about getting feedback in the first place. The most important thing to bear in mind is asking for it in advance. If you spring a request for some constructive critique on your audience after the event, you're putting them on the back foot. It's unlikely that they will have been watching with a view to giving you their detailed opinion, so you'll tend to get less actionable insights. When you request feedback in advance the person giving it to you can watch your delivery with this in mind, ensuring that what they go on to share is much more meaningful.

Choosing who you ask to evaluate your performance is worth giving some thought to as well. In a pitch context there may be formal paths to requesting feedback but if you're presenting at work or for a specific event, think about who will be in the audience whose opinion you would value. Ask people with more experience than you or who have a particular perspective that might be interesting. If you know someone is sceptical of the ideas you are sharing for example, it could be interesting to understand how your message landed with them. If you're presenting as a team and asking the audience for their opinion feels inappropriate, you can always ask your team members to keep an eye out for certain things too.

You also need to be specific about what you are asking for feedback on. This will help the person you ask to look at your presentation through the most useful lens. Do you want their thoughts on the structure? Are you looking for specifics around the visuals? Do you want to know how the stories and case studies landed? Or are you more interested in your performance and how you built rapport. Be clear on what their focus should be. It is more effective to have different people feeding back on different aspects rather than asking one individual to cover it all.

When the time comes for people to share their opinions, don't be afraid to ask for clarification to help you understand exactly what they're talking about. Avoid justifying your choices or trying to rebut what they are saying. Use open questions to aid your understanding of their perspective and then thank them for their input. It's important that you can make an informed decision as to whether you will take the feedback onboard. People's opinions are obviously subjective and only you can decide what to act upon and what to ignore. The more precise you were in your request, the more likely what they say will be useful. Don't dismiss anything immediately, take time to sit with it, look for patterns and reflect.

It's then important to capture your key insights so that you can carry the learning forward.

Build your presentation bank

Developing your skill as a presenter takes time. You have to put in the reps. You have to learn from your success and your failures. As part of the DEBRIEF phase it's therefore important to be as strategic as possible. What do you want to take forward next time? What do you want to ensure you avoid. Two things I encourage clients to create are a 'presentation bank' and a 'learning log'.

Think of your 'presentation bank' as a storage space for your greatest hits. What are the elements that worked well or sections that you might be able to recycle and reuse? There's no point continually reinventing the wheel. If you create a personal introduction that works, write it down. If you use a case study that resonates, capture it. If you design a slide that simplifies a complex idea, make a copy. Personally, I have a Master Deck with lots of individual elements that I may want to utilize in the future so that everything is one place. It's not about using the same material for every presentation you give. It's about refining and polishing the key ideas you need to communicate so that when you come to use them in the future you know exactly where to look.

Your 'learning log' is a list of the key lessons from each presentation and a rolling action plan for what you want to work on. It's too easy when life is busy to get hyper focused on the task at hand. Creating a 'learning log' mean that each time you come to present you can zoom out and choose which elements of your craft you would like to pay attention to. Keep coming back to this document regularly as you perfect your technique and approach. The best presenters never stop learning, so your log will also serve as great record of your journey.

 STAND & DELIVER

• •

CAPTURE YOUR LEARNING

When the pressure is on, wasting hours searching through old presentation files for something you want to reuse is frustrating to say the least. Trust me I've been there! Instead, I recommend creating your filing system up front. If you use a particular note-taking software, use that, but at the very least, create the following files and start to populate them.

Presentation bank – script ideas

This is a text document where you can dump all the script elements you are likely to want to reuse or modify in the future. Personal introductions, case studies, stories, interesting facts, phrases and explanations that worked. Label each item to make it easy to search for in future.

Presentation bank – slide ideas

Create a master document in whatever slide software you use, so that you can copy and paste key slides into it. I know professional speakers who have decks containing hundreds of slides that they can pick and choose from, then adapt as necessary depending on the audience and the context.

Learning log

This is a place to capture important feedback and learnings from your presentations. I also recommend you have a page to track the specific things you want to focus on as you develop your presentation and pitching skills. It's great to be able to tick them off or strike them through to chart your progress.

• •

Chapter summary

This sixth and final step of the playbook is about continuous improvement. How do you learn from every pitch and presentation you deliver, so that you continue to hone your skills? The more systematic you are in reviewing your performance and asking for feedback the quicker you build your technique. It doesn't have to be an onerous process, and it definitely isn't one you should skip.

For each presentation your deliver take time to do the following:

- ✓ Schedule review time in your diary to ensure it happens
- ✓ Use a review framework to capture your thinking
- ✓ Ask for feedback in advance of your presentation to make it more meaningful
- ✓ Be specific about what you want the person giving you feedback to focus on
- ✓ Create a 'presentation bank' to capture elements you might recycle and reuse
- ✓ Keep a 'learning log' of any useful feedback and action items you want to work on

In reality, the whole process I've laid out in this playbook is a continuous loop. Once you DEBRIEF your current presentation you take those learnings into the DISCOVER phase of the next one and the whole cycle repeats itself.

It's now time to take your learning and put it into action.

Epilogue
Action! Taking the next step

You now have the complete playbook for a pitch or presentation that will cut through the noise. You know the power of combining simplicity, emotion and energy to craft a message that will stay with your audience long after you have left the room. You understand the initial things you need to DISCOVER, the core ideas you need to DISTIL, the type of message you need to DESIGN, the process you need to DRILL, the skills required to DELIVER and the importance of making time to DEBRIEF. But it's all just theory until you step out of your comfort zone and put it into practice.

I'd love to be able to promise you that because you've read this book every pitch and presentation you deliver from now on will be perfect. But that would be misleading and unfair. Just because you have great tools doesn't make you a master craftsperson. And even master craftspeople have bad days! Your job now is to build your skill using the tools and ideas I have shared. To challenge and augment them. To stress-test them. To make them your own.

My hope is that there are elements from this playbook that you will use every single time you present. I'm also pragmatic enough to know that you won't put it all into practice immediately. By all means, choose the things you think will give you the quickest wins but don't neglect the rest. Keep coming back to each of the steps and refining your approach.

One of the best ways to embed new learning is to share it with others, so take the ideas contained within this book and spread them. It will deepen your understanding and you'll be helping other people in the process. As we established right at the beginning, life's a pitch. So, these are skills worth developing whatever you do for a living.

Pitching and presenting is a set of muscles you can build. You want both strength and flexibility. Like acting and directing I see it as a craft. Something that you continually develop and refine. That's part of what makes it fun. With effort and determination, you will begin to internalize the techniques. Things that felt clumsy will feel effortless. Elements that required deep thinking will become instinctive. I've been using the ideas contained within these pages for over 15 years and I'm still learning. But much of what I've shared has now become second nature. That's when things become exciting. That's when you experience cut-through. If you put in the work, I'm confident that you will experience it too. I wish you every success on your journey.

Acknowledgements

When I wrote *IMPACT*, I discovered that bringing a book into the world is most definitely a team sport, not a solo endeavour. The same has been true this time round.

The first person I need to thank is Laura, my gorgeous partner in life and business. Whilst I've been locked away at the bottom of the garden writing, you've held the fort and kept everything else moving. I couldn't have done it without your reassurance and love.

To my wonderful Nell, sorry for missing so many bedtime stories. I hope you'll be proud to read Dad's words in the future, and I'm so looking forward to getting back to *Lord of The Rings*! To our crazy Golden Retriever Brae, thank you for insisting that I walked away from my desk come rain or shine. The fresh air and exercise made my thinking and my writing clearer.

To my family, thank you for your unwavering support. Mum and Dad, your belief in me helps me believe in myself. Abbie, Ben, Fran, Zoe, Eli, Nico, Max, Ada, Jane, Jamie and Kyle your encouragement and love mean everything.

Emma, thank you for juggling my diary and finding me the time (even when it didn't look possible) to sit down and write. To the team at In Flow and all our wonderful trainers, thank you for helping spread the word and create more cut-through.

To my publisher Alison and the team at Practical Inspiration, thank you for taking a chance on this idea and helping me make it a reality. Out of House, I love the cover. Susannah, your early edits helped make everything flow. Christian, your video editing skills transform my content. Lisa at Pepperdog Design, thanks for helping me bring the models and illustrations to life, I always value our collaboration.

To my team of amazing beta readers – Lauren, Lynda, Mary, Matt, Naomi and Nick – your suggestions and feedback helped me to focus on exactly what matters to the audience. I owe you all a debt of gratitude.

Thanks also to all those who have read the manuscript in advance and have written such fabulous words of praise. It's incredibly humbling to have people whom I hold in such high regard endorse the methodology in this book and my expertise. A special thank you to David Hieatt for writing the Foreword. Your challenge and support throughout the writing process have been invaluable, and without our conversations, the whole idea would still just be an unscratched itch.

Finally, I want to thank all my clients, past delegates, readers of *IMPACT* and those who subscribe to my newsletter and YouTube channel. You have trusted me to be your guide and allowed me to test my ideas in the real world. I have learned so much from working with you and creating for you. I hope you find Cut-Through valuable and I look forward to hearing how you have used the tools and techniques.

With gratitude,
Dominic

Appendix A
More formulas for a
1.2.3. middle

Sometimes your *1.2.3.* middle section needs a more tailored approach. Below you will find ten formulas that can be used for the most common pitch and presentation scenarios that my clients ask for help with. Use the questions as prompts to help you craft your content.

1. Frustration – Improvement – Transformation (FIT)

Suggested use: Sales pitch

▶ **Frustration:** What are the problems, frustrations and pain-points that your product or service solves?

▶ **Improvement:** How could things be better? What needs to change?

▶ **Transformation:** How can you position your offering as the solution? How will it help the prospect?

2. Features – Advantages – Benefits (FAB)

Suggested use: Product demo

▶ **Features**: What are the product features most relevant to the user? How do they work? What makes them unique?

▶ **Advantages**: What makes the product superior? How is it different to the alternatives?

▶ **Benefits**: What will the user gain by using the product? What value does it provide?

3. Accomplishments – Challenges – Expectations (ACE)

Suggested use: Team update

▶ **Accomplishments**: What are the biggest achievements since the last update?

▶ **Challenges**: What obstacles have the team faced? Have they been overcome or are they still live?

▶ **Expectations**: What needs to happen next? Who is owning the action steps?

4. Progress – Roadblocks – Outlook (PRO)

Suggested use: Project review

▶ **Progress**: What has been accomplished so far? What milestones have been reached?

▶ **Roadblocks**: What are the challenges and obstacles currently being faced?

▶ **Outlook**: Are you optimistic everything is on track? What are the next steps and priorities?

5. Risk – Opportunity – Impact (ROI)

Suggested use: Business case

▶ **Risk**: What are the current threats being faced? What happens if no action is taken?

▶ **Opportunity**: What is the potential upside of the proposal? How can you quantify the advantages?

▶ **Impact**: What potential benefits would the decision bring? What outcomes can be expected?

6. Aspiration – Impact – Motivation (AIM)

Suggested use: Town hall/all-hands meetings

▶ **Aspiration**: What is the strategic direction, vision or big goal?

▶ **Impact**: How will the work that people are doing contribute to the big picture? What will the impact be?

▶ **Motivation**: What are the reasons people should act? How can you motivate them to take ownership?

7. Scope – Execution – Timeline (SET)

Suggested use: Project kick off

▶ **Scope**: What are the goals and deliverables of the project?

▶ **Execution**: How will the work be carried out? Who will be accountable?

▶ **Timeline**: What are the key milestones and any deadlines that are being worked to?

8. Mission – Action – Progress (MAP)

Suggested use: Strategy presentation

▶ **Mission**: What is the overarching goal and purpose?

▶ **Action**: What are the critical steps required to implement the strategy?

▶ **Progress**: How will success be measured and reported to ensure momentum?

9. Goals – Reflections – Opportunities (GRO)

Suggested use: Performance review

▶ **Goals**: What has been achieved so far? What progress has been made towards the agreed goals?

▶ **Reflections**: What went well? What can be improved?

▶ **Opportunities**: What are the next steps and priorities?

10. Learn – Explore – Do (LED)

Suggested use: Educational presentation

▶ **Learn**: What is the key idea or theory you want to teach?

▶ **Explore**: What examples or case studies do you have? What evidence backs it up?

▶ **Do**: What is the real-world application? How can your audience put theory into practice?

The author

A specialist in sales and leadership communication, Dominic Colenso has spent the last 15 years working with individuals and businesses around the world to help them speak and perform under pressure. A sought-after keynote speaker, trainer and coach, his YouTube videos and TEDx talk have had over two million views.

Beginning his career as a professional actor, Dominic worked extensively on stage and screen before training as a director at the Royal Academy of Dramatic Art in London. Performing in many of the UK's leading theatres, including the National Theatre and the Royal Court, he has appeared on film in everything from BBC period dramas to big-budget action movies. He is best known for playing the role of Virgil Tracy in the Hollywood adaptation of Thunderbirds, with Bill Paxton and Sir Ben Kingsley.

Dominic's experience and fascination with how the body, breath and voice can influence performance led him to set up his communication skills training consultancy, In Flow, and to write his first book IMPACT: *How to be more confident, increase your influence and know what to say under pressure*.

For all speaking, training and coaching enquiries please email info@dominiccolenso.com

Find Dominic online at:

 www.dominiccolenso.com

 www.linkedin.com/in/dominiccolenso

 www.youtube.com/@dominiccolenso

Notes

INTRODUCTION

1 Microsoft. 'Will AI Fix Work'. *Microsoft.com*, 9 May, 2023. Web. www.microsoft. com/en-us/worklab/work-trend-index/will-ai-fix-work. Accessed 18 May, 2025.
2 Web. https://dictionary.cambridge.org/dictionary/english/cut-through. Accessed 18 May, 2025.
3 VandeHei, Jim, Mike Allen and Rory Schwartz. *Smart Brevity: The power of saying more with less.* John Murray Business, 2023.
4 Colenso, Dominic. *IMPACT: How to be more confident, increase your influence and know what to say under pressure.* Rethink Press, 2019.
5 Covey, Stephen R. *The 7 Habits of Highly Effective People*. Simon & Schuster, 1989.

DISCOVER

1 Colenso, Dominic. 'Anna Hemmings'. *Why Life's a Pitch Podcast.* 4 October, 2023. Podcast. https://podcasts.apple.com/gb/podcast/anna-hemmings-beating-the-odds-with-9-gold-medals/id1708183978?i=1000630146373. Accessed 18 May, 2025.
2 Pink, Daniel H. *To Sell is Human*. Canongate, 2013.

DISTIL

1 Miller, George A. 'The Magical Number Seven, Plus or Minus Two: Some Limits on our Capacity for Processing Information' *Psychological Review*, vol. 63, 1956: pp. 81–97.
2 Lancaster, Simon. *Winning Minds*. Palgrave Macmillan, 2015.
3 Jobs, Steve. 'Steve Jobs Introducing The iPhone At MacWorld 2007'. *YouTube. com*, Web. www.youtube.com/watch?v=x7qPAY9JqE4. Accessed 18 May, 2025.

4   Cialdini, Robert B. *Influence.* Harper, 2007.

5   Web. www.forbes.com/sites/charliefink/2018/08/31/the-elevator-pitch-for-the-lion-king-true-story/. Accessed 18 May, 2025.

6   Campbell, Joseph. *The Hero with a Thousand Faces.* New World Library, 2008.

DESIGN

1   South Palpmares, Jennifer K. and Young, Andrew W. 'Facial First Impressions of Partner Preference Traits: Trustworthiness, status, and attractiveness.' *Social Psychology and Personality Science*, vol. 9, no. 8, 2018.

2   Miller, Donald. *Building a Story Brand.* Harper Collins Leadership, 2017.

3   Kahneman, Daniel. *Thinking, Fast and Slow.* Penguin Books, 2012.

4   Gates, Bill. 'Mosquitos, malaria and education'. *ted.com*, February, 2009. Web. www.ted.com/talks/bill_gates_mosquitos_malaria_and_education. Accessed 18 May, 2025.

5   Reynolds, Garr. *Presentation Zen Design.* Pearson Education, 2010.

6   Jackson, Lee. *Get Good at Slides.* Get Good Books, 2019.

7   Jackson, Lee. *Get Good at Slides.* Get Good Books, 2019.

DELIVER

1   Nestor, James. *Breath.* Penguin Life, 2021.

DEBRIEF

1   Rolfe, Gary, Dawn Freshwater and Melanie Jasper. *Critical Reflection in Nursing and the Helping Professions: A user's guide.* Palgrave Macmillan, 2001.

Also by Dominic Colenso

I f you've enjoyed *Cut-Through* you'll love *IMPACT: How to be more confident, increase your influence and know what to say under pressure*.

> 'A step-by-step process for increasing your self-confidence and finding your voice in any situation.'
>
> Daniel Priestley,
> bestselling author and award-winning entrepreneur

When you speak do others listen?

Does your message land?

Do people act upon your words?

In business and in life, great communication is the key to getting exceptional results. If you want to be more persuasive, have more gravitas and build better relationships this book will show you how.

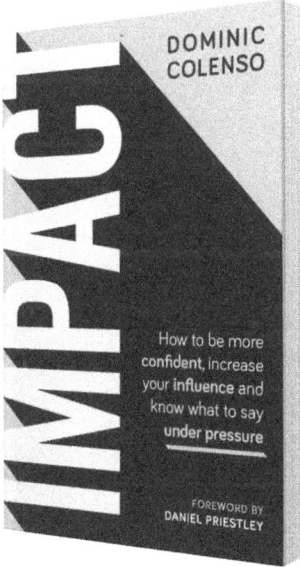

Index

Note: page numbers in *italic* type refer to Figures; those in **bold** type refer to Tables.

A quick word from Practical Inspiration Publishing...

We hope you found this book both practical and inspiring – that's what we aim for with every book we publish.

We publish titles on topics ranging from leadership, entrepreneurship, HR and marketing to self-development and wellbeing.

Find details of all our books at: www.practicalinspiration.com

 ## Did you know...

We can offer discounts on bulk sales of all our titles – ideal if you want to use them for training purposes, corporate giveaways or simply because you feel these ideas deserve to be shared with your network.

We can even produce bespoke versions of our books, for example with your organization's logo and/or a tailored foreword.

To discuss further, contact us on info@practicalinspiration.com.

 ## Got an idea for a business book?

We may be able to help. Find out about more about publishing in partnership with us at: bit.ly/PIpublishing.

Follow us on social media…

 @PIPTalking

 @pip_talking

 @practicalinspiration

 @piptalking

 Practical Inspiration Publishing